THE REIGN OF ELIZABETH I

THE REIGN OF ELIZABETH I

Carole Levin

palgrave

First published 2002 by
PALGRAVE
Houndmills, Basingstoke, Hampshire RG21 6XS and
175 Fifth Avenue, New York, N.Y. 10010
Companies and representatives throughout the world

PALGRAVE is the new global academic imprint of
St. Martin's Press LLC Scholarly and Reference Division and
Palgrave Publishers Ltd (formerly Macmillan Press Ltd).

ISBN 0–333–65865–5 hardback
ISBN 0–333–65866–3 paperback

This book is printed on paper suitable for recycling and
made from fully managed and sustained forest sources.

A catalogue record for this book is available
from the British Library.

Library of Congress Cataloging-in-Publication Data
Levin, Carole, 1948–
    The reign of Elizabeth I / Carole Levin.
        p. cm.
    Includes bibliographical references and index.
    ISBN 0–333–65865–5 (cloth)
    1. Great Britain—History—Elizabeth, 1558–1603.   2. Elizabeth I, Queen
of England, 1533–1603.   3. England—Civilization—16th century.   I. Title.

DA355 .L459 2001
942.05′5′092—dc21
    [B]   2001034815

10   9   8   7   6   5   4   3   2   1
11 10 09 08 07 06 05 04 03 02

Printed in China

For

Annie and Julie, Morgan and Nikki

and

Andrea, Debbie, Karolyn, Michele, and Stephanie

and

Carmella, Carolyn and Christine

CONTENTS

ACKNOWLEDGEMENTS

The following brief study is an introduction to Elizabeth I and her reign, attempting to place her rule within the context not only of her time, but also of our own. I have used the work of many fine recent scholars to synthesize the material, and those who are interested in going further or finding other interpretations and perspectives will find guides in the notes to each chapter. To make the work more accessible to a wide audience, the spelling throughout has been modernized.

In the last decades there has been a whole company of scholars who have brought new perspectives to Elizabeth and her reign, and who have brought to the forefront the importance of gender and culture in the early modern period. I am grateful to this scholarly community and have learned much from them. I would like particularly to thank Jo Eldridge Carney, Jane Donawerth, Ronald Fritze, Michele Osherow, and Bill Spellman for their care in reading the manuscript and the helpful suggestions that they made. Debbie Barrett-Graves, Al Geritz, Rick, Casey and Matt Gershon, Nancy Kassop, Elaine Kruse, Mary Ann Lee, Pamela Nickless, Lena Cowen Orlin, Charlene Porsild, Joe and Julie Silvestri, Lynn Spangler, and Pat Sullivan have supported the scholarship and much else.

I want to acknowledge the expert and thoughtful help of the librarians at Love Library at the University of Nebraska, especially Gretchen Holten Poppler and Kathy Johnson, and in Special Collections, Mary Ellen Ducey and Carmella Garman. Much of the work was done for this study at the Folger Shakespeare Library. I am deeply appreciative to all the staff there, but most especially to Louis B. Thalheimer Reference Librarian Georgianna Ziegler, whose amazing knowledge is only equal to her generosity.

I would like to thank the Research Council of the University of Nebraska-Lincoln for the support that allowed me to do some of the research for this study. I appreciate the helpfulness and efficiency of the editors at the publishers. My thanks to Penny Simmons for the copy edit, and to Ruth Elwell and Rohana Kenin for providing the index. My colleagues and students at SUNY/New Paltz and since 1998 at the University of Nebraska-Lincoln have matched my enthusiasm, and their questions and comments have helped me crystallize my thoughts. Especial thanks go to my research support network, or "goals group," Emily Greenwald, Mark Hinchman, and Julia McQuillan. Timothy Elston's support as both graduate student and teaching assistant were particularly valuable.

My great hope, expressed in the dedication, is that future generations of women will continue to enjoy studying and learning about Elizabeth I and her reign.

INTRODUCTION

Elizabeth I chose as her motto the Latin phrase, *Semper Eadem*, which means "Always the same." It is an ironic statement in many ways. During her reign many perceived Elizabeth as indecisive and changeable; after her death historians have regarded Elizabeth and her reign from a variety of different perspectives. As we move into the twenty-first century, we need to re-evaluate this enigmatic sixteenth-century Queen and the significance of her reign. Elizabeth I is one of the most famous women in history and one of the best known British monarchs. It is difficult to separate the myth from the reality of her reign, and each age brings its own values to an evaluation of her and her significance. The recent film *Elizabeth*, as well as the characterization of the Queen in *Shakespeare in Love*, have given a new generation ideas about Elizabeth and her age, some of which are interesting but have doubtful historical value. Certainly Elizabeth I was far more complex and effective than her depiction in the recent film that bore her name.

The reign of Elizabeth I was a time of incredible importance and of change not only in England but in Europe. One of the major issues was religion, as England under Elizabeth finally became a Protestant nation, and there were great pressures on Elizabeth to go to the aid of other Protestants in Europe and to fight against Catholicism. Though Elizabeth tried to keep England at peace, by the end of the reign England was involved in a war with Catholic Spain. At the same time, England was truly finding its own national identity and it was a time of great cultural development. In the final decade of Elizabeth's reign the work of such writers as William Shakespeare, Edmund Spenser, and Christopher Marlowe flourished.

Elizabeth's reign was also significant in terms of changing gender expectations and attitudes about those who were different. Explorations, trade, and the first steps of colonization marked the Elizabethan era, resulting in the beginnings of what would eventually become a much more diverse population in England as a whole, but especially in its

1

capital city, London: a very small community of Jews, though they did have
to outwardly practice Anglicanism; some Africans as household servants,
court entertainers, interpreters for trading companies, and prostitutes.[1]
This was also a time of superstition and accusations of witchcraft. At the
same time that a woman was ruling, other women, often at the bottom of
the social scale, were accused and hung as witches.

The interest in Elizabeth I, Queen of England from 1558 to 1603, seems
to be unending, as are the interpretations of her reign. While her motto
was "Always the same," in fact there are many different ways to view this
powerful sixteenth-century female monarch.[2] Some of the earliest bio-
graphical portraits of Elizabeth appear in the work of her contemporaries: in *Acts and Monuments,* first published in 1563, John Foxe described
Princess Elizabeth as at risk during the reign of her sister Mary, and how
she was saved by God's intervention for the good of England. Early in
the seventeenth century William Camden, a headmaster at Westminster
School and a professional historian, produced his *The History of the Most
Renowned and Victorious Princess, late Queen of England*, a history of the reign
up to 1588 published in Latin in 1615, with English translations in 1625,
1628, and 1635. The section on the final part of the reign was not published, at his request, until after his death since it mentioned many
people still living. His work strongly defended Elizabeth's achievements.
Foxe and Camden presented strongly positive Protestant perspectives,
in contrast to the harsh views presented by Elizabeth's contemporaries,
such Catholics as Cardinal William Allen and Edward Rishton, who
wrote condemning her during her reign.[3]

Religious ideologies continued to have a strong impact on the way
Elizabeth was viewed even centuries after her death. For example, during
the nineteenth century both Protestant James Froude and Catholic John
Lingard were critical of Elizabeth, but from different points of view.
Lingard described Elizabeth as someone who tried to rule as an absolute
monarch; she was an arbitrary tyrant who was vain, excessively suspicious,
and had a terrible temper. While Lingard's hostility may well have
developed because of Elizabeth's treatment of Catholics, James Froude's
criticisms of Elizabeth stemmed from what he perceived as her indiffer-
ence to Protestantism. He believed the successes of the reign were due
not to Elizabeth, but to the sound decisions of her Principal Secretary,
William Cecil.[4]

Throughout the twentieth century there has been scholarship on
Elizabeth. John Neale's studies of Elizabeth's Parliaments and his biography of the Queen are classics.[5] In the last decade or so a number of

new biographies and studies of aspects of her reign have appeared. They range from the harshly critical work of Christopher Haigh to the highly positive feminist view of Susan Bassnett. Wallace MacCaffrey's studies on her foreign policy have also resulted in a fine political biography of her. Very recently, Leah S. Marcus, Janel Mueller, and Mary Beth Rose have produced a careful and thorough edition of her own writings.[6] As a result, we have seen a number of new interpretations and perspectives of the 44-year reign of this important English Queen.

The purpose of this brief study is to present a clear narrative of the major topics of Elizabeth's reign and to discuss the interplay among the political, religious, social, and cultural issues of the time, particularly in light of recent scholarship. In the sixteenth century, the relationship between politics and culture was dynamic and complex. Elizabeth's reign saw great cultural development that often reflected and helped interpret political events. This study presents a narrative of significant aspects of Elizabeth I's reign that takes into account the most recent scholarship and interpretations.

The first chapter narrates Elizabeth's life, and provides the reader with a chronology of important events throughout her reign. The religious settlement and the struggles between Catholics and Puritans are the focus of Chapter 2. Chapter 3 examines England's foreign policy under Elizabeth in the first part of her reign. Despite problems in France and Spain, Scotland and Ireland, England was able to keep herself, at least in part, in peace – if an uneasy one. Chapter 4 examines the foreign policy in the later part of the reign when that peace crumbles and England is finally at war with Spain. Both chapters examine not only England's relationship with the Continent, but also within the British Isles, particularly English efforts to dominate Ireland. Chapter 5 looks at the difficult issue of the succession, and the various plots and rebellions against Elizabeth. Chapter 6 examines the shifting nature of English society and culture in the last decade of her reign, and the difficulties for Elizabeth and England at a time of war and economic distress. Yet the 1590s were also a time of amazing cultural achievement. In all these issues Elizabeth both got advice from, and struggled with, pressures from both her Privy Council and Parliament, which are discussed throughout the text where appropriate.

In examining the reign of Elizabeth, one finds the major issues are all interconnected and overlapping; thus religion has a great deal to do with concerns over foreign policy as well as anxiety over the succession. Mary Stuart, Queen of Scots, for example, is discussed in different contexts in a number of the chapters. Elizabeth's cousin, the Catholic Scottish Queen, stood in counterbalance to Elizabeth; she was the potential heir, and the focus of rebellions and plots, and had impact on England's foreign relations with not only Scotland, but France and Spain as well.

The interplay of religion and politics, notable in the reign of Henry VIII, continued throughout the second half of the sixteenth century. Looking at the major themes of Elizabeth's reign allows us insights into the life and reign of a remarkable woman, and a remarkable time in history.

1

OVERVIEW OF ELIZABETH'S LIFE AND REIGN

In early September 1533 Henry VIII was not the only one to eagerly anticipate the birth of his child by his second wife, Anne Boleyn, nor the only one to hope that this child would be a son. Everyone in England, and, indeed, Western Europe, was waiting. Henry would eventually have a son, Edward, but his short, unhappy reign would be eclipsed by the long and far more successful reign of his sister, Elizabeth. Her success demonstrated that Henry's belief that he must have a son to secure England's safety was misplaced. Nonetheless, Henry's desire for a male heir was understandable; we may, however, question if his anxiety justified his six marriages and the beheading of two of his wives.

Henry had become king in 1509, a few months before his eighteenth birthday, and only the second Tudor to succeed to the throne after the tumultuous Wars of the Roses of the fifteenth century. Though the number of people who actually died in that conflict was relatively small, it was in the popular, public memory a time of terror and lawlessness. Henry's father, the first Tudor monarch, Henry VII, ruled more by right of conquest after his victory over Richard III at the battle of Bosworth Field, than by the right of primogeniture, though he established an elaborate claim to the throne based both on his Lancastrian claims and his connection to the mythical King Arthur. Henry VII also developed the perspective that Richard III was God's scourge and he, Henry, was God's agent sent to remove him.

In the early years of his reign Henry VII battled further Yorkist claims and pretenders, and though he and his wife Elizabeth of York, oldest daughter of Edward IV, had had three sons, both Arthur, his eldest son, and Edmund were dead when Henry VIII became King. Henry VIII was all too aware of the chaos that could come were there not a stable succession.

Upon becoming King, one of Henry's first acts was to marry his older brother Arthur's widow, Catherine of Aragon, daughter of Ferdinand and Isabella of Spain. Catherine had been in England in a terribly ambiguous situation since the death of her young husband only five months after the marriage seven years before. Henry VII had obtained a dispensation so that his son could marry his dead brother's widow, but he also had the young Henry swear he was not bound by this proposed marriage. Though Henry VIII claimed it was his dying father's wish that he marry Catherine, the choice seems to have been his.

And in many ways Catherine was an ideal wife to Henry; she was highly educated, loyal, and strong willed. But she failed at her premiere function as Queen; she had no son who survived infancy. Their only surviving child was Mary, born in 1516. In the early 1520s it was obvious to everyone there would be no more pregnancies for Catherine, and by 1527 Henry began to explore the possibility of having his marriage annulled, a not unusual situation for kings.[1] But it was complicated in this instance by a number of issues, such as Catherine's own international political connections, and her refusal to accept the premise that she was not Henry's true wife. Catherine was the aunt of Charles V, Holy Roman Emperor and King of Spain, and Charles was the last person Pope Clement VII wanted to offend. Clement had to deal with both the threat of Lutheranism sweeping through much of Western Europe, and the emperor's armies conquering and occupying Rome in 1527, just as Henry was negotiating with him for a divorce from Catherine. Henry's passion for Anne Boleyn, a lady at his court, and his determination to marry her rather than make another political match, added to the complexities.

The power of Charles V, and Pope Clement's fear of him, led the Pope to procrastinate, hoping that somehow the situation would resolve itself. Clement did offer Henry the possibility of a new dispensation so that he could either have two wives at once or else marry his daughter Mary to his illegitimate son, Henry Fitzroy, the Duke of Richmond, but Henry refused to accept either of these dubious alternatives. By 1529 Henry was impatient enough to jettison his long-time advisor Thomas, Cardinal Wolsey. This was to prove to be the first tentative step toward the break with the Church of Rome and the establishment of an independent Church of England with Henry himself as its Head.

Henry needed some authority to help him carry out his divorce, and in November 1529 Parliament was summoned. This Parliament was unprecedented. It met for seven years, enacted 137 statutes, 32 of which were of national significance, and was involved in the affairs of Church in a manner no earlier Parliament had ever anticipated. The Reformation Parliament was not only of vital importance in itself: it established a precedent about the role of Parliament that Elizabeth was to find very difficult in her dealings with her own Parliaments.[2]

At first Henry expected to use Parliament, with its many anticlerical members, to terrify the English clergy and the Pope, and cause the Pope to accede to Henry's desires because of the increasing anticlerical legislation. But Clement still refused to grant the annulment, and by 1533 Parliament declared "this realm of England" to be an empire, and neither Pope nor Emperor could tell its King, or its people, what to do. Moreover, Parliament decreed that all spiritual cases should henceforth be under the jurisdiction of the King of England. His new Archbishop of Canterbury, Thomas Cranmer, appointed after the death of Archbishop William Warham in August, 1532, then declared Henry's marriage to Catherine null and void, and Henry openly proclaimed his marriage to Anne Boleyn, who was five months pregnant at the time. Her coronation was one of exceptional magnificence. Henry had broken with the Catholic Church and turned his whole world upside down to have a legitimate son; however, the child to whom Anne Boleyn gave birth on 7 September 1533 was another daughter.

The marriage of Henry and Anne ended brutally in Anne's execution for adultery before Elizabeth's third birthday. Elizabeth, like her older sister Mary, was declared illegitimate. After her mother's execution Elizabeth's childhood was difficult. Henry's third wife Jane Seymour gave Henry the son he craved. Elizabeth faded into the background, though she was occasionally at court to greet her father's various new wives. Henry's marriage to his sixth and last wife, Katherine Parr, in 1543 briefly brought some stability to Elizabeth's life, and Katherine was an important model for Elizabeth of a pious, able Queen.[3] The same year an Act of Parliament reinstated both Mary and Elizabeth in the succession, though the Act did not remove the stigma of illegitimacy. Henry's will in 1546 confirmed Elizabeth's position: if Edward were to die without heirs, the throne would pass to Mary; if she were to die without heirs, to Elizabeth. For good measure, after Elizabeth, the Stuart line descended from Henry's older sister Margaret was excluded and the Suffolk line descended from his younger sister Mary was placed next in line. Though

Henry's will excluded the Stuarts, Margaret's granddaughter Mary Queen of Scots would be the dangerous alternative Queen for much of Elizabeth's reign.

From the time she was a child Elizabeth received an extensive education; scholars from Cambridge were chosen to teach her who were clearly situated in the reform movement. At first she had some instruction from her brother Edward's tutors, Dr Richard Cox and Sir John Cheke. In 1544 William Grindal became her own private tutor. He was an expert not only in Latin, but also in Greek, both of which he taught Elizabeth. She also became fluent in French and Italian. Elizabeth translated Margaret of Angoulême's *Mirror of the Sinful Soul* for Katherine Parr as a New Year's gift in 1545. The following year, Elizabeth translated Katherine's own private prayers into Latin, French, and Italian as well as providing a translation of John Calvin's *How We Ought to Know God*. In 1546 Elizabeth stayed permanently at Court under Katherine's supervision.[4] Elizabeth's education was not, however, intended to befit her for ruling should this event take place. Unlike her brother Edward, she never received a course in the problems of practical politics given by the Clerk of the Council, William Thomas. After she became Queen, Elizabeth told her Parliament that she had studied nothing but divinity until she herself became a ruler, "then I gave myself to the study of that which was meet for government."[5] In fact, however, the dangerous political waters Elizabeth successfully navigated in the reigns of Edward VI and Mary were excellent training for her.[6]

Henry VIII died at the end of January 1547 and young Edward succeeded to the throne; Elizabeth, then aged 13, went to live in the Queen Dowager Katherine Parr's household. After what many saw as an indecently short period of widowhood, Parr secretly married Thomas Seymour, the youngest of the new boy-King's maternal uncles, in April or early May. Seymour took his nephew, Edward VI, into his confidence and gained his support. Though Seymour's older brother Edward, Duke of Somerset and Lord Protector, was furious, nothing could be done when the marriage was made public, and Thomas moved into the Queen Dowager's household at Chelsea. Seymour's relationship with the young Elizabeth became more and more familiar; he would come into her bedchamber in the mornings and tease and sometimes tickle her, sometimes slapping her on the bottom. The presence of Elizabeth's governess Katherine Ashley kept the situation from getting completely out of control, and though Elizabeth seems to have enjoyed bantering with the Lord Admiral, she soon began to rise earlier so she was dressed and at her studies when he appeared. At first Katherine Parr dealt with the situation that developed between her husband and stepdaughter by joining in on the teasing, but after she became pregnant and unwell Parr began to be concerned. Early in 1548 she suggested that Elizabeth leave her household and set up her own at Cheshunt with Sir Anthony Denny and his wife. Though Elizabeth may have been upset at first, she soon realized the wisdom of the Queen Dowager's decision; Elizabeth's relations with Katherine and Seymour remained cordial and she corresponded with them.

The situation became more tragic as well as more dangerous for Elizabeth, however, when Parr died of complications due to childbirth in September 1548. Seymour began to think about marrying the young Elizabeth, a plan that Katherine Ashley unwisely encouraged, though it would have gravely angered Edward VI's Council and possibly jeopardized her place in the succession. During the fall of 1548, Thomas Seymour engaged in a number of other unwise and illegal activities, including piracy, coining false money, and eventually considering kidnapping his nephew Edward. In January 1549 he was arrested on the charge of high treason and lodged in the Tower. Elizabeth's governess, Katherine Ashley, and her cofferer, Thomas Parry, were also arrested and examined; in their terror they told all about the goings on at Chelsea.

The Council sent Sir Robert Tyrwhitt to examine the 15-year-old Elizabeth to find out her role in Seymour's various plots. Elizabeth handled herself so well and carefully that she managed to extricate herself from the crisis and protect her servants, Ashley and Parry, though Seymour was executed in March 1549. After the Seymour affair Elizabeth dressed with ostentatious simplicity and, later in Edward's reign, came to court and showed herself – very consciously self-fashioned – as the ideal modest Protestant young woman. This behavior, argues Mac-Caffrey, "suggests her determination to present an image of maidenly modesty and decorum." The Protestant martyrologist John Foxe, in some ways ironic, given Elizabeth's dress once she became Queen, lauded her while she was princess for her "little pride of stomach," her "little delight ... in gay apparel, rich attire, and precious jewels."[7]

The other pivotal force in her life at that time was her tutor Roger Ascham, one of the leading scholars of his generation and confirmed in his Protestant beliefs. After Grindal's death from the plague in 1548, Elizabeth chose Ascham to be her tutor, and she flourished under his care. In 1550, the year he ceased to be Elizabeth's tutor, Ascham wrote to a friend, Jacob Strumm, "She has just passed her sixteenth birthday, and her seriousness and gentleness are unheard of in those of her age and rank. Her study of the true faith and of good learning is most energetic. She has talent without a woman's weakness, industry with a man's perseverance."[8] Taught by Ascham for about two years, she acquired the elements of a serious classical education. Fluent in Latin, competent in Greek, she read Isocrates and Sophocles in the morning and Cicero and Livy, the Church Fathers, and the New Testament in the afternoon. In addition, she studied history, theology, philosophy, and the other sciences that comprised the advanced curriculum of the day. Elizabeth also learned to play the virginal and the lute and enjoyed listening to music. She was also riding and hunting and, though we have no specific record of it, was most probably trained to dance; by the time she became Queen she was dancing effectively and with much pleasure in what was called the Italian manner.

Elizabeth was welcomed at Edward's court in 1549 and again in 1551. By the time of the second visit, the power at court had shifted. The Duke of Somerset had lost his position of power to John Dudley, Duke of Northumberland. Somerset followed his brother Thomas Seymour to the block in January 1552. But Northumberland's power depended on the King and young Edward's health was growing more problematic.

After Edward's death in July 1553, Elizabeth managed to avoid the entanglement of Northumberland's unsuccessful plot to overturn Henry VIII's will by having the next ruler be Edward's cousin Lady Jane Grey, recently married to Northumberland's youngest son.[9] Her older sister Mary welcomed Elizabeth to Court. On 3 August Elizabeth rode behind Mary in the procession when the new Queen entered London. This cordiality was, however, short-lived. Mary was steadfast in her Catholicism and her desire to restore England to Rome. Mary listened to the Spanish Ambassador, Simon Renard, who gravely distrusted Elizabeth. Elizabeth, conscious of the need to keep the support of Protestants, was at best half-hearted in her conversion to Catholicism; this angered Mary enough that Elizabeth left court to live in the country. Mary assured intimates that Elizabeth physically resembled Mark Smeaton, reputed to be one of Anne Boleyn's lovers, more than Henry VIII; the Queen also gave other women, such as her cousin Margaret, Countess of Lennox, precedence over Elizabeth at court. Elizabeth not only had to suffer Mary's ill will; she was also confronted with those who saw her as a natural alternative to the Catholic Queen, whose policies and plans to marry Charles V's son, Philip of Spain were disturbing to many of the English. Though we have no evidence that Elizabeth was involved in any plots, she seems to have been unwillingly aware of such conspiracies, and her experience as Mary's heir convinced her not to name an heir of her own once she was Queen. By January 1554, the time of Thomas Wyatt's rebellion against the Queen's coming marriage to Philip of Spain, Mary was convinced that Elizabeth had known and approved of the plot against her. She demanded that Elizabeth return to court to answer questions about that involvement. Mary also ordered the execution of her cousin Jane Grey and her husband; they had been lodged at the Tower since the failure of the Northumberland coup. Jane's execution further terrified Elizabeth. Though Elizabeth was unwell, Mary would take no excuse, and Elizabeth made the journey to court, though as slowly as she dared. The Spanish Ambassador, Renard, and the Lord Chancellor, Stephen Gardiner, Bishop of Winchester, wanted Elizabeth sent directly to the Tower, but there were a number of members of Mary's Council who opposed this plan.

Elizabeth was held for nearly a month in her rooms in Whitehall. Wyatt and his fellow conspirators were thoroughly examined, but there was no clear evidence that the princess was involved. Mary and her Council argued over what to do with her. No one was willing to guard Elizabeth under house arrest and Gardiner convinced the Council that she should be sent to the Tower. While he could not convince them to put her on trial for treason, he hoped that while she was in the Tower more evidence would emerge.

As a result, Richard Radclifffe, the Earl of Sussex, and a colleague, possibly the Marquis of Winchester, were sent to take Elizabeth to the Tower by barge, as Mary and her Council feared there might be attempts to rescue her if they took her through the streets of London. Elizabeth was extremely distraught by the news and asked that she might see her sister Mary before such an order was carried out. When this request was refused, she begged for paper and pen so that she might at least write to Mary. Sussex overrode his colleague and allowed Elizabeth the time to write to her sister. MacCaffrey points out that writing this letter "was a measure of her desperation but also her personal shrewdness."[10] Elizabeth's letter beseeched her sister to allow her to see her before being imprisoned in the Tower, a place from which she was afraid she would never emerge. Elizabeth hoped that if she could actually see and talk with her sister, her professions of innocence would save her. The letter, however, only gained Elizabeth one day before she was sent to the Tower. Elizabeth's letter writing meant they missed the tide, and Sussex was concerned that taking the barge at midnight was too dangerous – in the dark Elizabeth might escape. Mary was furious with Sussex that he allowed her sister to write, and she refused Elizabeth's fervent plea to see her.

The next morning, Palm Sunday, 17 March 1554, when people in London were at mass so they would not be there to either rescue Elizabeth or demonstrate against her imprisonment, she was conveyed to the Tower. It was raining. Elizabeth landed at the gate later known as "Traitor's Gate" but then called "the watergate." At her landing there was a great multitude of servants and warders standing at attention. According to Foxe, Elizabeth took advantage of this audience to proclaim before her entrance to the Tower, "Here lands as true a subject, being prisoner, as ever landed at these stairs; and before thee, O God! I speak it, having no other friends but thee alone." Her mood then shifted. Elizabeth paused for a moment outside the gate and sat on a stone, even though it was damp with rain. The Lieutenant of the Tower, Sir John Bridges, asked her to come in: "Madame, you were best come out of the rain, for you sit unwholesomely." Elizabeth responded: "It is better sitting here than in a worse place, for God knows, I know not whither you will bring me." Seeing and hearing Elizabeth thus, one of her gentlemen ushers began to weep. Elizabeth scolded him that this was not comforting, and besides no one need weep for her, for she was innocent.[11] Whether the young Princess actually had the presence of mind to say all this, and whether years later, Foxe actually got her words exactly right, Elizabeth's subjects would have had this dramatic moment firmly placed in their minds, as Foxe's *Acts and Monuments* was one of the most popular books of its age. It was also a useful statement to be made to those whose job it was to see her into the Tower. Sussex reminded the others that Elizabeth was after all the daughter of Henry VIII, and had best be treated fairly.

Sussex was not the only strong supporter Elizabeth had. Mary did not want to alienate Lord Admiral William Howard, Elizabeth's maternal great-uncle, by trying Elizabeth for treason on insufficient grounds. Elizabeth's position was also strengthened on 11 April 1554, when Thomas Wyatt stated from the scaffold to the crowd about to witness his death that Elizabeth had had no knowledge of his rebellion. Gardiner hoped that Parliament would agree to disinherit Elizabeth, but Lord Paget convinced a reluctant Mary that it would be wiser to dissolve Parliament than to bring forward such a contentious issue.

It became more and more difficult to justify Elizabeth's imprisonment in the Tower, and in May the Council prevailed upon Sir Henry Bedingfield to keep her under constraint at Woodstock. The four-day trip from London demonstrated all the more how popular Elizabeth still was: all along the route people thronged forward to catch a glimpse of her and to offer her cakes and other treats. While in Woodstock, Bedingfield took great pains to keep Elizabeth from seeing anyone except her servants, and infuriated Elizabeth even more by dismissing Elizabeth Sands, one of her favorites. He also refused to allow Elizabeth to have an English Bible, presenting her with one in Latin instead. After Mary was angered by one of Elizabeth's letters, for some months Bedingfield refused to allow her to write again either to the Queen or the Council.

But while Elizabeth was in the country, much was going on at court. Philip arrived in July and soon after, he and Mary were married. By November Mary was convinced she was pregnant; she was equally delighted that her cousin Cardinal Reginald Pole, the newly arrived papal legal, absolved England from its repudiation of Rome, opening the way for the formal restoration of papal authority. But Mary's pregnancy proved to be an illusion and the restoration with Rome all too soon brought with it the persecution of heretics. From February 1555 until her death in November 1558, around 300 people were burned to death, about 60 of them women.

Despite Elizabeth's very realistic fears for her own safety as well as her place in the succession, she did survive her sister's reign to become Queen at Mary's death in November 1558. Eventually, in part due to Philip's intervention, Elizabeth visited court and then was allowed to retire to Hatfield with her household. As much as Philip might have distrusted Elizabeth, the alternate heir, Mary Stuart, living at the French court and betrothed to the Dauphin, was even more problematic. Mary, Elizabeth's Catholic cousin and Queen of Scotland, was the granddaughter of Henry VIII's older sister Margaret, and, by primogeniture, the next heir after Elizabeth. In fact, for some Catholics Mary had a better right to the throne than Elizabeth since the Pope had never recognized the nullity of Henry VIII's marriage to Catherine of Aragon, thus making Elizabeth a bastard. Elizabeth might not be an ideal solution from Philip's point of view, but at least she was not the future daughter-in-law to the French King, his enemy.

While Philip failed to convince Mary I that she must force Elizabeth to marry Emmanuel Philibert, Duke of Savoy, she did at his behest declare war on France in June 1557. The war was a disaster, and the port city of Calais, England's last holding from the Hundred Years' War was finally lost. This military defeat only added to the demoralization England was feeling as Mary's reign drew to a close. On 6 November 1558, the seriously ill Mary finally listened to the demands of her Council and formally named Elizabeth her heir – something all but the Queen had long assumed. Less than two weeks later, on 17 November Mary died and Elizabeth was now Queen of England.

In 1558 the country had a surprisingly smooth transition to Elizabeth, given the crises that had happened only five years earlier when Edward VI had died and Mary's hostility to Elizabeth as her heir. But though there was a rush of relief over the death of Mary and the endings of the fires at Smithfield that had burned heretics, there was also deep anxiety over whether the reign of a 25-year-old woman would be any more successful. Many of the English, distressed by Mary's religious persecution and losing the war with France, were delighted with their new young Queen, though some worried that her reign would be short and chaos would follow. While Catholic Mary had ruled, Elizabeth had been the hope of the reformers, a hope that was only partially justified from their perspective once she actually became Queen. Her accession was only a few months after the publication of the Scots Calvinist John Knox's *The First Blast of the Trumpet Against the Monstrous Regiment of Women*, and Elizabeth's reign saw a continued debate, that had begun with Protestant pamphlets from the mid 1550s, on whether a woman ought to rule. As John Guy argues, "Many contemporaries found the prospect of female rule terrifying."[12]

Elizabeth began her reign emphasizing the theme of national unity. While Elizabeth may have hated her half-sister and all she stood for, Elizabeth did not try to settle any old scores, or allow those who had come back into power to do so either. She wanted to be Queen of all the English, not just the Protestants. She wanted a united aristocracy behind her and managed to rally most of them to her cause, succeeding "to a remarkable degree."[13] She wanted to be Queen of an independent England, to encourage old industries to grow and to develop new industries so the country would no longer be so dependent on imports from abroad, and to encourage trade. She wanted to be Queen of a strong England that could stay at peace and not feel threatened by the great Catholic powers on the Continent, France and Spain.

One of Elizabeth's first acts was to appoint William Cecil, whom she had known since the time she lived in Katherine Parr's household, as her Principal Secretary. Eventually he achieved the title of Lord Burghley and the office of Treasurer. She had other loyal servants, including Sir Francis Walsingham; Sir Christopher Hatton; Richard Ratcliffe, the Earl of Sussex; John Whitgift, appointed Archbishop of Canterbury in 1583; and Sir Robert Dudley, eventually Earl of Leicester. Her relationship with Dudley was based on personal affection, and for a number of years he tried, though unsuccessfully, to convince her to marry him. Dudley was the son of the executed traitor John Dudley, Duke of Northumberland, who had once been the most powerful man in the realm. Robert Dudley's close relationship with Elizabeth, and the influence that it gave him, meant he had many enemies; throughout her reign scandal surrounded Elizabeth concerning the actual nature of her relationship with Dudley.

William Cecil's relationship with Elizabeth was very different from that of Dudley, and often, especially early in the reign, Cecil worried about the other's influence, that Dudley might marry the Queen himself, or keep her from marrying someone Cecil thought to be more appropriate. Elizabeth had a long and fruitful partnership with Cecil. He greatly influenced the shape of foreign policy from 1558 to 1572 while he was Principal Secretary. When he became Lord Treasurer and Baron Burghley, and Walsingham succeeded him as Secretary from 1573 to 1590, Elizabeth still consulted Cecil on foreign as well as domestic policy, and most ambassadors and agents continued to correspond with him as well as with Walsingham. Elizabeth did not recruit her very closest advisors simply because they shared her views. She argued for years with Cecil over what to do with Mary Stuart, and for a long time disagreed deeply with Leicester and Walsingham about what should be England's policy towards the Netherlands. Despite their enduring political relationship, Cecil and Elizabeth had serious disagreements, particularly over the question of what limitations, if any, there were on the sovereignty of the ruler, and how bound she was by the advice of the Privy Council.[14]

On matters of policy, Elizabeth consulted most often with Burghley, Walsingham, and Leicester, though other councillors also played a part, and at various times during her reign each felt that he was not properly consulted. For much of her reign, the different points of view of her advisors did not harden into factions. In the 1570s and 1580s Walsingham, with the support of Leicester and Hatton, pushed for a more aggressive and Protestant foreign policy, something which Burghley had also supported in the 1560s although in the following decades he had become more cautious. On this issue Burghley was supported by Whitgift and Sir Walter Mildmay. But Burghley was in alliance with Walsingham and Leicester as they attempted to support and protect the

Puritans as the reign progressed. In this they were countered by Hatton and Archbishop Whitgift. The differences between Burghley and Walsingham were for the most part ones of emphasis: they agreed about what should be done, but differed on how and when.[15] These various men who, at different times, were close advisors to Elizabeth also served on her Privy Council, which was an important place for making policy. By the end of Henry VIII's reign the Privy Council had established its importance to the monarch: it advised the ruler on policy, carried out responsibility for general administration and public expenditure, and coordinated the work of the different agencies of government. The Council met to discuss matters of state and to present advice to the monarch. In Elizabeth's case this advice was presented later; after the first month of her reign Elizabeth met with it only sporadically, preferring to consult with her advisors singly or in small groups.[16]

When Elizabeth became Queen, she dismissed about two-thirds of Mary's Privy Council; her own Council was smaller, about 18, and the men on it worked well together. When Elizabeth became Queen, she appointed to the Council men she could trust, such as Cecil, Nicholas Bacon, and Thomas Parry. In her attempts to reach consensus, she also kept some of the more moderate, as well as powerful, of Mary's Catholic councillors in office, such as the Earls of Arundel and Shrewsbury.[17] At the beginning of Elizabeth's reign, about half of the members of the Privy Council were nobles. As the reign progressed that group declined in number, as Elizabeth replaced them with her most trusted courtiers. By the end of her reign her council had only 11 men. Whitgift was the only bishop who was ever on the Council in the entire reign. The Council worked hard; it usually met several times a week, and by the 1590s it was meeting almost every day, mostly to deal with issues about the war with Spain. The Secretary of State, the most significant of those to hold the office being William Cecil, Francis Walsingham, and Robert Cecil, organized the Council's affairs and reported to the Queen and to the other departments of government. Elizabeth found in dealing with such issues as the religious settlement or the succession that members of the Council, if they failed to convince her, would turn to Parliament for support in pressuring her.

Parliament had a great deal of authority through its enactment of statutes. Parliament made and repealed laws, established forms of religious devotion, and set taxes. By the mid-sixteenth century many regarded it as, in the words of the contemporary Sir Thomas Smith, "the most high and absolute power of the realm of England."[18] But that power was still controlled by the monarch, who alone could summon, prorogue, or dissolve Parliament. Without the monarch's consent, no statute could become law. Though today we think of the House of Commons as the more important, in the sixteenth century the Lords considered themselves the more significant; their members were certainly more politically powerful and had more prestige in terms of social rank. There were somewhere between 65 and 80 who sat in the House of Lords. In the last Parliament of Henry VIII's reign, 343 sat in the House of Commons. In 1601, the last Parliament of Elizabeth's reign, it was 462. Penry Williams argues that the number grew as the Crown tried to find places for useful men in Parliament. Elizabeth was not packing the House of Commons, but getting in men who could help in the complicated matter of managing the business at hand.[19] But though it had its power, Parliament, like her Privy Council, frequently failed to compel the Queen to act as it wanted. MacCaffrey points out the significance of Elizabeth's decision making: "every move in the complex interplay of events was hers." Christopher Haigh suggests that "she used the power of her personality, and the fierce personal loyalty she was able to evoke, to dissolve the political alliances which sometimes sought to coerce her."[20]

Elizabeth had many issues with which she struggled with Parliament and her Council. One of the most important, as well as the most immediate, to deal with once she became Queen was religion. After the constant changes the English people had seen in regard to religion, Elizabeth attempted a broadly based compromise, but as her reign progressed she had to resist pressure on it from both sides: Catholics and Puritans. While she was able to work well with some members of the church hierarchy, and had a particularly fruitful relationship with her last Archbishop of Canterbury, John Whitgift, she had problems with many of her bishops. Some of her bishops felt Elizabeth did not support them adequately, while she mistrusted the more zealous Protestants among them. She was in especial conflict with Edmund Grindal, who became Archbishop of Canterbury in 1575 with the support of both Burghley and Walsingham. The conflicts became so intense that in 1577 Elizabeth ordered that he be suspended from exercising his office. While he was not dismissed as archbishop, the suspension was never lifted; effectively, the Church had no active leader until his death in 1583 when he was replaced with Whitgift. Her problems with Catholic resurgence also became far more intense after the first decade, once her cousin Mary Stuart arrived in England in 1568, having fled Scotland after her forced abdication.

Mary Stuart's presence in England complicated another significant issue with which Elizabeth had to deal: the succession. From the beginning of her reign, Elizabeth's Council and Parliaments beseeched her to marry. They were eager for Elizabeth to have a son and settle the succession, and many of them found the idea of an unmarried woman ruling unnatural.[21] Though William Cecil maintained a long and trusted relationship with Elizabeth, especially at the beginning of the reign, her refusal to commit to a marriage frustrated him greatly. He wrote about it frequently to his contemporaries, at one point fretting, unless she got married, "as now things hang in desperation, I have no comfort to live." He also prayed that "God send our mistress a husband, and by him a son, that we may hope our posterity shall have a masculine succession." Norman Jones argues that "Cecil's frustration with unmarried female rulers probably went beyond the politics of the moment, for it was common knowledge that there was something unnatural about a woman ruler. Weaker vessels in need of management, women in positions of command inverted the natural order instituted by God."[22]

Elizabeth, however, while she played with courtship and perceived its value as a useful political tool, in the end refused to marry; she also would not name an heir. The example of Henry and his succession of wives would hardly have convinced Elizabeth that marriage was an enviable estate or that even if she married, she would have a surviving son or survive the rigors of childbirth herself. Elizabeth had a variety of suitors: her former brother-in-law, Philip II; Philip's cousin, the Archduke Charles; the Scottish Earl of Arran; Eric XIV of Sweden; and the sons of Catherine de Medici, both Henry Duke of Anjou (later Henry III); and Francis, Duke of Alençon, later Duke of Anjou. While at the beginning of her reign there was a strong popular interest in Erik of Sweden, Elizabeth expressed no interest in him; she also quickly declared it was impossible to think about marrying Philip.

Elizabeth's favorite, Robert Dudley, to whom Elizabeth eventually gave the title Earl of Leicester, was also a forceful suitor for her hand. For years rumors swept around Elizabeth and Dudley, particularly after the mysterious death of his wife Amy Robsart in 1560.[23] Elizabeth may have seriously considered marrying Dudley in 1560, but William Cecil led the opposition in the Council, seeing Robert's ambition as a menace both to the Crown and to England, and Elizabeth soon came to realize how potentially politically disastrous such a marriage could be. There was also bitter controversy over two other serious foreign suitors, the Hapsburg Archduke Charles in the 1560s and the French prince Francis,

Duke of Alençon, later of Anjou, in the late 1570s, early 1580s, since both were Catholics. But if no one could agree on the right husband for Elizabeth, and she had no child of her own, the succession was unsettled. Elizabeth's brush with death in October 1562, when she contracted smallpox, forcefully made clear how dangerous it could be to the realm if Elizabeth died without heirs. Though Elizabeth claimed God would take care of England, her subjects thought she should provide some care as well.

The problems of religion and the succession were interconnected, especially since Elizabeth remained unmarried and refused to name an heir. By primogeniture, Elizabeth's Catholic cousin Mary Queen of Scots was the next heir, and, some believed, the rightful Queen. Scotland and England had been at odds for centuries, as England had attempted to dominate Scotland, who in return had looked to France for help. When James V died while Mary was still an infant, the English saw this as a great opportunity to gain Scotland by taking control of Mary and eventually arranging a marriage between her and Edward VI. Instead, her mother the Regent Mary of Guise shipped Mary off at the age of five to be raised at the French court and eventually be the consort of Francis II. While in France Mary quartered the English arms to demonstrate that she was the rightful Queen. But upon Francis's death in December 1560, Mary returned to Scotland the next August. Her 1565 marriage to her cousin Henry Stuart, Lord Darnley, however, proved disastrous; he allowed himself to be manipulated into a plot against Mary and helped murder her Italian secretary David Rizzio. After the birth of their son James in 1566, Mary wanted no more to do with him. Her next marriage to James Hepburn, Earl of Bothwell was even worse since he was the reputed murderer of Darnley, who in February 1567 had been found strangled in his garden after Kirk o' Field, the Edinburgh house where he had been staying, had been blown up. Mary's marriage to Bothwell only a few months later led to a rebellion against her as people suspected she collaborated with Bothwell in her husband's murder. She was captured and forced to abdicate in favor of her infant son. Mary refused to repudiate her marriage to Bothwell, though later she would ask the Pope for an annulment. In May 1568 Mary managed to escape and fled to England, presenting Elizabeth's government with what seemed an insoluble problem.

Elizabeth did not want to return Mary to Scotland as Queen with full power, nor did she want to see the Scots execute Mary. Allowing her to go on to France or Spain might mean that Mary would return to Scotland with an army, which could then be turned against England. Therefore

Elizabeth felt she had no choice but to keep Mary in confinement. It turned out to be for 19 years. Her presence in England undermined the delicate religious balance, leading to the Northern Rebellion in 1569 headed by the earls of Northumberland and Westmoreland and to Elizabeth's excommunication by papal bull in 1570. During Mary's captivity there were a number of plots to assassinate Elizabeth, free the Scottish Queen, and place Mary on the English throne with the aid of foreign invasion. In 1572 Thomas Howard, the Duke of Norfolk, was executed for his role in the Ridolfi Plot of the year before. Conspirators had hoped to free Mary, marry her to Norfolk, and crown them King and Queen of England after Elizabeth and Cecil were assassinated with the aid of 6000 troops sent over by the Duke of Alva in the Netherlands. By 1884 Protestants were so upset over the Scottish Queen that they formed the Bond of Association, where signatories threatened Mary with death if Elizabeth was assassinated. The Babington Conspiracy of 1586, yet another attempt to assassinate Elizabeth with Mary's complicity, finally led Elizabeth to reluctantly sign Mary's death warrant; the Scots Queen was executed on 8 February 1587.

The problems with Mary Stuart demonstrated the impact of religious division on international politics. There were other issues. The English were extremely concerned about the Spanish army in the Netherlands, and from 1584 onward Elizabeth publicly supported the Protestant rebellion in the Netherlands with not only money, but also men. Mary Stuart's execution helped to convince Philip of Spain that he could conquer England and restore it to Catholicism without having a French Queen as a result. Philip finally committed himself to the invasion; in the summer of 1588 after a number of delays, he launched the Armada. Against the advice of some of her councillors that she should stay safe at court, Elizabeth went to Tilbury Camp to encourage the assembled troops. A combination of English naval skill and bad weather foiled the invasion.

In a number of ways, the final 15 years of Elizabeth's reign after the defeat of the Armada were difficult. The advisors she trusted most died. To her great personal grief she lost Robert Dudley, Earl of Leicester, in 1588. Elizabeth locked herself in her room for days. Walsingham died in 1590. Burghley's death in 1598 was also especially difficult for Elizabeth. The economy suffered from the drain of the long and expensive struggle in Ireland that had been going on since the 1560s, but finally reached crisis proportions in the later 1590s as the Earl of Tyrone lead a rebellion. The continued support in the Netherlands was also costly. These foreign policy expenses were especially problematic as the 1590s suffered from bad harvests and inflation. Continued struggles with Puritans over the religious settlement were also divisive. In 1594 Elizabeth's physician Roderigo Lopez, of Portugal Jewish background though outwardly an Anglican, was accused of planning to poison the Queen and executed. That spring Christopher Marlowe's play, *The Jew of Malta*, was put on, frequently to sell-out crowds. The anti-Jewish sentiment was paralleled by a belief that the relatively few Africans in England were one cause of the economic problems because they were taking jobs away from the English. The 1590s also saw a number of witchcraft prosecutions.

Another serious problem was the struggle for power of some of the younger men at court for Elizabeth's favor, and the factions, with clear ideological components, hardened in a way that was detrimental to Elizabeth's ability to rule.[24] Her relationship with her last favorite, Robert Devereux, Earl of Essex, stepson to the Earl of Leicester, was especially difficult, and he perceived himself as the enemy of William Cecil's son Robert, and of Sir Walter Raleigh. While Cecil saw England's position as more one of defense, Essex believed his country's natural role was the champion of Europe against Spain at whatever cost. Alternately Essex cajoled and threatened Elizabeth in an effort to gain power and get his way on policy and for rewards for his followers. Essex led a disastrous campaign in Ireland to subdue rebels. The disgrace he faced when he returned to England without leave eventually led him to stage a rebellion against the Queen in 1601. It failed, and Essex was executed.

But a flowering in literary cultural development also marked the latter part of Elizabeth's reign. The work of such men as Edmund Spenser and William Shakespeare must have drawn inspiration from the extraordinary woman who ruled England both as a Virgin Queen and mother of her people. And while literature, and especially drama, was most remarkable, architecture, music, and portrait painting were also flourishing. Overseas trade was expanding and there was the beginning of interest in expansion and colonization, though this also signified the beginning of involvement in the slave trade.

Elizabeth aged visibly after the Essex rebellion and his subsequent execution. She held the final Parliament of her reign that same year. Though her physicians could not name a specific complaint, by the beginning of 1603 her health began to fail, and she died on 24 March 1603. Elizabeth had always refused to name an heir and stated God would take care of England. Though had she died earlier there might well have been strife and blood-shed, her cousin James VI of Scotland peacefully ascended the throne of England after Elizabeth.

2

RELIGIOUS DIVIDES AND THE RELIGIOUS SETTLEMENT[1]

When Elizabeth became Queen in 1558, English Christians experienced their fourth religious upheaval in a generation. Once Henry VIII had broken with the Pope, for the rest of his reign there had been a pendulum swing from the conservatives, who had wanted England to be Catholic in ceremony and doctrine but without allegiance to the Pope, to the reformers, who wanted to use the opportunity to see real change in liturgy and doctrine. With the death of Henry, the reformers had been given free rein, and the official church was extremely Protestant under Edward VI, only to return to Catholicism and obedience to the pope under Mary, though Mary's regime could not obliterate all reformist thought and action.

Despite all the changes there was quite a smooth transition to Elizabeth, though she had to face a country not only split between Catholics and Protestants, but with Protestants who had many different views about the true nature of the Church. The tensions between devout Catholics and the variety of ardent Protestants left many people confused and wary about discussing religion at all.

Historians today generally agree that Elizabeth wanted the official Church under her to proceed further in reform than it had under Henry VIII, but there is disagreement about what form of Protestantism she actually did want. It is difficult to know since many records do not survive and Elizabeth herself was extremely ambiguous about religion, as she was about so much else. Elizabeth's lack of clarity may have caused religious confusion, but, Norman Jones also suggests, allowed Elizabeth to gain a firm control over her realm. Elizabeth's dislike of religious enthusiasm caused her Catholic subjects to hope she might return to the fold and thus prevented a Catholic uprising or her excommunication by the Pope until over a decade into her rule.[2] But so many changes over a brief period caused not only confusion, but also some opposition. Mary had used her reign to give enough support to re-establishing Catholicism so that it made it far harder for her successor to abolish it. Some conservatives resisted Elizabeth's changes. The length and stability of Elizabeth's reign allowed these changes to become more permanent and settled. A number of scholars now believe that the real break with traditional Catholic practices for most of the population did not occur until about halfway through Elizabeth's reign in the late 1570s or early 1580s. Before 1559, hostility to the traditional Church and strong committed feelings about Protestant ideas were confined to a small section of the population. But while there might have been relatively few reformers, they placed themselves in positions where they could influence and lead policy.[3]

In 1559 Parliament defined the official religion of England and its relationship to the state in a series of statutes that began with Acts of Supremacy and Uniformity.[4] Catholic mass was yet again abolished. The Act of Uniformity returned England to the Edwardian Protestant form of worship and its passage through Parliament was even more difficult than that of the Act of Supremacy. The form of the new service determined by the Act of Uniformity was the 1552 Book of Common Prayer, with some alterations that made the mass vague enough that it would, as Norman Jones points out, "permit the sacrament of the Eucharist to be all things to all people, allowing them to understand Christ's words at the Last Supper any way they wished." The service was again in English, instead of the Latin of Mary's reign.[5] In 1563 Convocations, the assembly of clergy, produced the Thirty-Nine Articles, which provided the Elizabethan Church with a doctrinal basis. They were ratified by Parliament in 1571.

The Parliament of 1559 not only passed the Uniformity Act, setting forth the official doctrine of the Church of England, it also passed the Supremacy Act giving Elizabeth the title of Supreme Governor over the Church of England. Henry VIII and his son had been called "Supreme Head," which suggested more power and prestige, but in fact there was little difference. Yet, whether Elizabeth should be called "Head" or "Governor" caused a great deal of commotion. Some members of the House of Commons argued that it was against the word of God for Elizabeth to refuse to be "Head" of the Church; many reformers, as well as papists, however, did not feel that this was an appropriate title for a woman, that in fact it would be sacrilegious, and Elizabeth was under a great deal of pressure not to use it. Claire Cross suggests that Philip II's disapproval of the title might also have been a serious consideration for Elizabeth.[6] That people from a variety of perspectives opposed the idea of a female head of the Church may well have been the deciding factor in Elizabeth's decision to seek instead the title of Governor. When Supremacy was being debated in the House of Lords, Nicholas Heath, Archbishop of York, made an argument from a Catholic perspective that echoed the Scots reformer John Knox's *First Blast of the Trumpet Against the Monstrous Regiment of Women*. Heath stated that

> Her highness, being a woman by birth and nature, is not qualified by God's word to feed the flock of Christ, it appears most plainly... To preach or minister the holy sacraments, a woman may not... A woman, in the degrees of Christ's church, is not called to be an apostle, or evangelist, nor to be a shepherd, neither a doctor or preacher. Therefor she cannot be supreme head of Christ's militant church, nor yet of any part thereof.[7]

Elizabeth decided she did not want to be the Head of the Church, but rather its Governor, not because it was inappropriate because she was a woman, but that it would be wrong for anyone, man or woman, as it usurped Christ's place.[8] But though Elizabeth decided against the title, she was not willing to relinquish the power over the Church she believed to be hers by right. John Guy argues that "despite the purposeful ambiguity of the settlement of 1559," Elizabeth's position was not significantly different from Henry VIII's. While she might delegate the exercise of her authority, the power was hers alone and came immediately from God.[9] Elizabeth took being Governor of the Church very seriously, and, argues William Haugaard, "fought passionately to establish her vision of the national church."[10] Yet Elizabeth was also politically careful in her role as Supreme Governor, and instead of confronting the church hierarchy directly, forced her bishops to carry out the fight for the shape of the national Church. She also frequently expected them to do so without the official support that they needed, which must have caused them some problems. Matthew Parker, her first Archbishop of Canterbury, often found himself in a difficult situation, attempting to carry out Elizabeth's wishes without her public support.[11] The Act of

Supremacy also recognized the right of the Supreme Governor to delegate her authority in certain ecclesiastical matters to commissioners, and established a Court of High Commission, also known as the Ecclesiastical Commission. The commissioners were empowered to punish crimes against ecclesiastical law, to settle ecclesiastical disputes, and to enforce religious uniformity.

The difficulty Elizabeth's government had reimposing Protestantism reflects the ambivalence of many of her contemporaries who had already gone through a number of religious changes. As Jones points out, "Although the majority of the English still had traditional beliefs they did not agree on the Pope's right to lead them. Papists, as opposed to sacramental Catholics, were a minority. The supremacy passed easily and uniformity with difficulty."[12]

As Queen, Elizabeth regularly attended morning services in the royal chapel, and she wrote her own private prayers for her daily worship. While she did define herself publicly as a Protestant, Elizabeth also wanted some Catholic ceremonial and traditions within her Church, both for personal and for political reasons. She disliked married clergy. She loved elaborate Church music. She refused to believe that all images were idolatrous. She also wanted the Catholic powers to think she was not that different from them so they would tolerate her and not launch a Holy Crusade against England, and she wanted the Lutheran Princes in Germany to support her so did not want to appear too different from them. Some elements of the Church of England – such as vestments, crosses, and candlesticks – were similar to Catholic ritual. Elizabeth needed to reassure both Lutherans and Catholics that England was not a Calvinist country. And Elizabeth herself did not want an English Calvinist Church. The Royal Injunctions of 1559 were part of this policy. In 1560 Elizabeth sanctioned the use of a Latin Prayer Book in the universities and in the colleges of Winchester and Eton. Also at the beginning of her reign, she argued successfully with the Archbishop of Canterbury and other church leaders about her use of a silver crucifix and candles in her royal chapel. Elizabeth insisted that the clergy wear vestments that made them look as if they were Catholic priests, and she required that they continue many traditional ceremonies, such as the making of the sign of the cross in baptism and requiring parishioners to kneel for communion.

Historians have traditionally suggested that Elizabeth was a politique who was very knowledgeable about Christianity, but had little religious conviction. But more recently, the work of such scholars as William Haugaard, J. J. Scarisbrick, and Margaret Aston suggest far otherwise.

Elizabeth was not a zealot, and her refusal to give support upset many of the passionately committed Protestants of her reign. But Diarmaid MacCulloch is also right that Elizabeth took great care to conceal her personal religious attitudes, so it is now difficult to know exactly what she preferred.[13]

Norman Jones argues persuasively that Elizabeth got what she wanted in the Church Settlement of 1559, and that its passage – the Act of Uniformity passed by only a three-vote margin in the hostile House of Lords even if Supremacy passed easily – was a triumph for both Queen and Commons. G. W. Bernard agrees that, in understanding the nature of the Church of England after the Elizabethan Settlement, one has to take seriously into account "the preferences, intentions, and compromises" of Elizabeth, and that she deliberately fostered compromise and ambiguity in the settlement. "Any view of the Church of England that fails to give due weight to its 'monarachical' element is thus misleading," he concludes.[14] But it is also probably true that having arrived at that Settlement, Elizabeth was satisfied, even if she did not find it to be ideal, and wanted it left alone. She did not desire the thorough reform in the Church that many of her divines wished. This was probably wise not only because of Elizabeth's own inclinations, but because, a number of historians now argue, on her accession the majority of the population was still Catholic in belief in terms of their theology, though not necessarily in terms of obedience to the Pope. Elizabeth's Protestant regime had to convince the people to leave their traditional beliefs and, through preaching and education, really convert the country to Protestantism. Elizabeth's government was outstandingly successful at this task. By the end of her 44-year reign only about one to two percent of the population was still Catholic. Though fear of Catholicism continued well into the seventeenth century, in fact that religion had little impact by the end of the Queen's reign.[15] Elizabeth may well have believed that bringing her subjects to Protestantism would be easier if the Church Settlement they had to accept was not so different in ritual from the old ways. In temperament, though clearly Protestant, she was also more sympathetic to Catholics and less to Puritans.

The Church played an important role in encouraging patriotism. The homily against rebellion, which was to be read frequently on Sundays in church, used many stories from the Bible demonstrating that rebellion against the sovereign was a sin against God, and the people's primary duty was obedience. The frontispiece to the 1569 Bishops' Bible was an illustration of the Queen. John Walter suggests of the Elizabethan Church "that it came perilously close to devoting as much time to the worship of Elizabeth as to the worship of God."[16]

The majority of Elizabeth's subjects, whether secretly Catholic in perspective or not, obediently attended Church on Sundays since they could be fined a shilling for non-attendance. And the ceremonies of the Church of England had probably been deliberately designed so that some Catholics could comfortably come to church as required by law. But the Catholic gentry could afford the fine, and certainly those seriously committed to the Catholic Church did not simply give in without a struggle at the beginning of Elizabeth's reign. The bishops that Mary had appointed fought against the Elizabethan Settlement and all but one of the Marian episcopate refused to take the Oath of Supremacy. About one hundred fellows and other senior members left the University of Oxford in the first decade of the reign; a number of them went into exile abroad. Some academics went to the Catholic University of Louvain, where they published many books of theology. By 1564 Louvanist attacks on the Elizabethan Church were being smuggled into England. Two years later Elizabeth was so concerned about the illicit importing of foreign works that she recommended that boats landing in England be searched for Catholic books. Some parish priests followed the example of their bishops. Approximately 300 of them refused to take the Oath of Supremacy and were deprived of their livings. Seventy to 80 of them went into exile, and at least 130 suffered terms of imprisonment at one time or another; around 30 priests died in prison. During the 1560s the Pope and the Catholic Church hierarchy did all it could to encourage Protestants to become Catholic and to convince Catholics that it was wrong to attend Protestant church services. In that decade many deprived Marian priests were active, especially in Yorkshire and Lancashire, saying the mass to the faithful as well as providing such functions as celebrating prohibited feasts and hearing confessions. There were also many Marian priests who stayed in their posts, but did not completely conform to the official Church, and kept alive a number of Catholic rituals and practices: Catholic altars, rosary beads and holy water, mass for the dead, revering images.

In the 1560s Elizabeth preferred persuasion instead of coercion against her Catholic subjects. She hoped that Catholicism would wither away as the older generation of Catholics died off and the supply of priests dried up. Elizabeth also probably realized that coercion would not be effective, since in some parts of the country, such as Yorkshire, three-quarters of the leading families were Catholic. Elizabeth and her government usually only took vigorous action if people openly defied the law.

Elizabeth circumvented the 1563 legislation which imposed the death penalty on anyone who twice refused the Oath of Supremacy by telling her Archbishop of Canterbury Matthew Parker that if someone did not take the oath the first time, they should not be asked a second time. The punishments for other offenses were also very lenient compared to the reigns of earlier Tudors. While making the decision not to persecute Catholics in the first decade of her reign allowed them to survive, it also did not push them to rebel. By the early 1570s the lay commitment to Catholicism was declining in many areas of England.

Unfortunately, despite the fact that the number of Catholics was diminishing, a number of people perceived Catholics to be more and more of a threat to the security to the realm. Mary Stuart's flight to England in 1568 after her forced abdication and the deteriorating relations with Spain made many people anxious. Pius V, Pope since 1566, referred to Elizabeth as one "who pretended to be Queen of England," and the year he became Pope he formally forbade Catholics in England to attend Protestant services.[17]

The next few years saw a number of domestic and international political crises which had severe religious overtones, causing even more fear of Catholic resurgence: the Northern Rebellion of 1569, and the bull of excommunication the following year, which denied Elizabeth's right to rule, relieved Catholics of their loyalty to her, encouraged her overthrow, and stated that, in the meantime, good Catholics must not attend their parish churches. Even more serious was the Ridolfi Plot in 1571, a plot to assassinate Elizabeth I and place Mary Stuart on the throne.[18] The second and greatly expanded edition of John Foxe's *Acts and Monuments*, commonly known as *The Book of Martyrs*, was published in 1570. Dale Hoak suggests that the timing of the publication was carefully coordinated with Cecil to respond to recent Catholic attacks on the sovereignty and integrity of Elizabeth's ruling of England.[19] Foxe's vivid descriptions of Protestant martyrs killed during the reign of Mary I gave emotional resonance to the dangers of Catholic resurgence.

Attacks on Protestants on the Continent also intensified fears of what Catholics might do to Protestants in England if the Catholics regained control. On St Bartholomew's Day, 24 August 1572, Catherine de Medici ordered the slaughter of thousands of Protestants. The English who heard about the massacre across the Channel were horrified. The Spanish agent Antonio de Guaras wrote to the Duke of Alva, "I have since heard that, whilst the Queen was hunting in company with her principle Councillors, the said post from France reached her and she read the letters at once, whereupon she immediately abandoned her hunting and returned to the palace, so distressed at the news that all the Court was downcast." For those actually in Paris witnessing the slaughter, the experience marked them forever. Walsingham, at the time ambassador to France in Paris, concluded of the French Catholics, "I think [it] less peril to live with them as enemies than as friends."[20] Many believed there was an international plot to wipe out Protestantism throughout Europe. The St Bartholomew's Day massacre not only horrified the English in itself, but reminded them that the same could happen if Catholics returned to power in England.

Elizabeth's problems with her Catholic subjects were interconnected with her relations with the powerful Catholic countries on the Continent, France and Spain. Persecution of recusants was always most severe when there were crises in international affairs. The political crisis of 1569–70 came at the same time that Catholics on the Continent were beginning to mount a determined missionary effort. Eventually, such missionaries as the Jesuit Edmund Campion, who returned to England in 1580 and was executed as a traitor in December 1581, determined they would combat heresy to the death if necessary. As relations deteriorated between England and Spain, particularly after 1582, strict penal laws allowed Catholics to be executed as traitors. The years of tacit toleration for the peaceable Catholic minority was ending. And there continued to be some Catholic plots to assassinate Elizabeth, such as the conspiracy led by Francis Throckmorton, arrested in 1583, and the supposed plot of William Parry's to murder Elizabeth as she walked in the gardens in 1585.[21] William Cecil publicly declared for the government that these people were condemned not for their religious beliefs, but for their lack of allegiance to the Queen, but this could be a very fine line for some devoted Catholics. In fact, however, the vast majority of Catholics in England were loyal to Elizabeth, and this became evident later in the reign when Philip II sent the Armada. They did not want to become subjects of Spain and recognized that the aim of bringing England back to allegiance to Rome was unrealistic. While there was still a small minority who held these goals, many Catholics believed their first loyalty was to their prince, in this case, Elizabeth.[22] By the mid-1590s the government began to perceive the Catholic threat as much less dangerous.

Elizabeth did not only have to contend with the issue of Catholics; though they publicly maintained their loyalty, in many ways Elizabeth had even less patience with the Puritans. Because the Elizabethan Church Settlement did not have a clear unified doctrine, some historians have traditionally described it as a middle ground between Rome and Geneva, the Pope and Calvin. This, however, may well be too neat and tidy an explanation that implies a clearly thought-out agenda. But pragmatic and politic considerations helped to shape the English Church under Elizabeth, and her clergy were never in complete accord with either her or each other. There were serious tensions not only between those who were not whole-hearted supporters of the new ways, but also between Elizabeth and members of her Church hierarchy that were never fully resolved. Moreover, England was also part of the European picture. Susan Doran argues that it is not accurate to use the term "Anglican" to describe the Elizabethan Church since it was not completely separate from the European Reformation.[23] Indeed, Christopher Haigh suggests "Elizabeth was perhaps the only determined 'Anglican' in England."[24]

Elizabeth was committed to the perspective that the Church had been established and there would be no more discussion; she refused to countenance what some Protestants considered to be further essential reform. She would not allow Parliament to discuss it further. She told the House of Commons in 1585, "Resolutely, she will receive no motion of innovation, nor alter or change any law whereby the religion or Church of England stands established at this day."[25] Elizabeth was also insistent that the clergy follow the established Act of Uniformity and Thirty-Nine Articles. Her efforts early in her reign to ameliorate Catholics into the body politic also offended a number of committed Protestants. Conrad Russell suggests that Elizabeth "settled for churches that looked Catholic, and sounded Protestant . . . This might have been a clever compromise . . . [but] most of the leading figures in Elizabeth's Church spent the reign itching to get rid of the half of the Church they thought did not belong . . . Elizabeth thus achieved what she wanted. Yet the fact remained that this was a Church with which no one was satisfied."[26]

Elizabeth's committed Protestant opposition has often been called Puritan, but more recently historians are realizing that the term Puritan is also not easy to define as Puritans were not a clearly identified subgroup.[27] The following discussion attempts to clarify the term as much as possible. Historians have used the term, however loosely, to refer to those Protestants who opposed the Elizabethan Settlement of 1559. In the latter part of Elizabeth's reign many people, themselves Protestants, used the term "Puritan" as a form of abuse. Those called Puritans would call themselves "the godly," and some historians use the two terms

interchangeably. That the label "Puritan" was used frequently in Elizabethan England is suggestive of the theological, moral, and social tensions of the time.[28] Patrick Collinson and Peter Lake define Puritans as
Protestants, both lay and clerical, who were much more intense in their
religious enthusiasm and zeal than their contemporary Protestants.
Their insistence on following what they perceived as a godly life separated them from their neighbors, who were Protestants who used the
term "Puritan" to denigrate. Puritans wished for a Biblical morality in
their own English society. Puritans were forcefully committed to purging
the established church of all its popish "superstitions" and wanted to see
the church stripped of external ornamentation. Rather than any visual
elements in church services, Puritans believed in the supremacy of the
spoken word and the importance of preaching and lectures. Because of
its emphasis on the word, Puritanism had less impact among the poor
and illiterate. In the countryside, many of the poorer people dismissed
the emphasis on the word of the Bible as "bibble-babble."[29] But if Puritans were less successful with the common folk, they enjoyed support
from powerful Court patrons. Some, but not all, Puritans refused to
accept the church hierarchy and believed in the Presbyterian system,
with each congregation having a minister but no bishops. Puritans
tended to be more anti-papal and more fundamentalist in their treatment of the scriptures than other Protestants. Puritans liked to not only
attend the parish church on Sunday mornings; later in the day they
would go to private meetings with other Puritans and repeat and learn
the lessons of the sermons. They would either read the Bible or Foxe's
Acts and Monuments. It was said that what distinguished a Puritan from
other Protestants was the unquenchable love for sermons. Puritans
ranged from moderates, some of whom were members of Elizabeth's
government, to radicals, who would never so compromise themselves.[30]

The term Puritan was first used in the mid-1560s to describe the
zealots who were upset with what they perceived as the conservatism of
the 1559 Prayer Book, and refused to conform to all the rituals so pre-
scribed there. Elizabeth refused to amend the Prayer Book, she enforced
conformity, she was reluctant to repress Catholics. She disliked preaching,
preferring that her ministers use government produced sermons or
"homiles" instead of creating their own. This led to struggles with the
radical Protestants, who felt Elizabeth put politics ahead of true religion.
When Edmund Grindal was Archbishop of Canterbury, he argued that
the homilies were better than nothing, half a loaf being better than none,
but, he suggested, "if every flock might have a preaching pastor, which is

rather to be wished than hoped for, then the reading of homilies would be altogether unnecessary." Elizabeth completely disagreed. She told Archbishop Whitgift and other bishops in 1585 that there was more learning in one of the homilies than in 20 of some of the sermons they and their ministers preached.[31]

Just as Puritans did not appreciate the homilies, the Prayer Book's conservative features disappointed both the returning religious exiles, who had been exposed to Reformed liturgy on the Continent, and radical Protestants who had joined underground sects in Mary's reign. As the years passed, and Elizabeth made it clear that she had no intention of modifying her Settlement, the initial disappointment become much more intense.

In 1565 Elizabeth ordered her church hierarchy to put pressure on ministers who would not conform to the ceremonies laid down in the Prayer Book. As the decade progressed, the pressures on nonconforming Protestants increased. In 1571 ecclesiastical authorities cancelled existing licenses to preach. They required ministers to state their agreement with the Prayer Book and the Thirty-Nine Articles before they could get new licenses. A number of ministers were, as a result, suspended and deprived of their offices. The same year, by order of the upper house of Convocation at Canterbury, Foxe's *Acts and Monuments*, one of the most popular books of its age, was placed in every cathedral church and every household of the Church hierarchy.

The Puritans the government found most dangerous were ones who attacked the church hierarchy and favored a Presbyterian form of organization. In the spring of 1570 at Cambridge, Thomas Cartwright, Lady Margaret Professor of Divinity, publicly criticized the episcopal nature of the Elizabethan Church in a series of lectures on the first two chapters of the Acts of the Apostles. John Field, a minister in London who was one of the leading Presbyterians, was soon repeating the call for reforms and was suspended.[32] Field's colleague Thomas Wilcox argued for an institution of a ministry of pastors, deacons, and elders to replace the hierarchical structure of the established Church in *An Admonition to Parliament*, co-authored with Field and published in 1572. Two years later Cartwright published an English translation of Walter Travers' *De Disciplina Ecclesiastica*, the *Book of Discipline*, describing what the Church should look like.

Elizabeth and the bishops were furious and appalled by Field and Wilcox, who were imprisoned at Newgate for a year. Cartwright fled to Heidelberg. Despite government attempts to suppress *An Admonition*, it was widely read. The book caused a breach among Puritans, however, as moderates were also shocked by the idea of destroying the church hierarchy. They were much more concerned with reform of the liturgy and believed that there was room for diversity of practice in ecclesiastical government. They saw the demands of Cartwright, Field, and Wilcox as divisive. Presbyterianism was developing, but it was to remain a marginal, though very disruptive, force within the Elizabethan Puritan movement.

The early Presbyterian leadership was centered in Cambridge and London; soon, however, the movement fanned out. Despite their radicalism, a number of important men at Court, such as Cecil and Dudley, provided the early Presbyterians with a measure of support and protection, because they saw them as a balance to the potential counter-Reformation against England. The papal excommunication and the waves of Catholic seminary priests coming into England and the example of the St Bartholomew's Day massacre seemed far more dangerous to a number of Elizabeth's advisors. As a result, the Presbyterian movement was not crushed at its beginnings, though Elizabeth and her Archbishop of Canterbury did their best to repress it.

This intense repression ended in 1575 with the death of Matthew Parker and the installation of Edmund Grindal, who had a different perspective on what the established church should be and his role as highest churchman. He hoped to introduce reforms himself and heal the divisions among Protestants. The Geneva Bible, which had not been printed in England as long as Parker was alive, went through 18 editions during Grindal's time as Archbishop. While some of the editions were obviously intended for private and domestic use, others, because of their size, could only have been intended for parish churches. Unlike the authorized Bishops' Bible, some editions contained puritanical versions of the Book of Common Prayer which omitted ceremonies that the Puritans believed to be doubtful, such as private baptism, confirmation, and the churching of women, which was a purification ritual for women to be accepted back into the church after childbirth. Grindal had been one of the Marian exiles and had very different ideas about the nature of the Church than Elizabeth. It soon brought the two into serious conflict.[33]

During Grindal's first year in office he strongly encouraged the ministers to take their preaching seriously, and saw to it that conformity was not widely enforced. But in 1577 a severe argument broke out between Elizabeth and Grindal over the issues of prophesying and meetings of clergy and laypeople to discuss preaching and scripture. Elizabeth was opposed to these meetings because she saw the potential in them for seditious preaching and was afraid they would be a means for radicals to influence other ministers. Grindal, on the other hand, believed this was the most effective way to train a preaching clergy, and he refused to obey her order to suppress these meetings. With more courage than tact, Grindal wrote Elizabeth a 6000-word letter, including the statement, "I cannot with safe conscience and without offence of the Majesty of God give my assent to the suppressing of the said exercises." He added, "Bear with me, I beseech you, Madam, if I choose rather to offend your earthly Majesty than to offend the heavenly Majesty of God," reminding the Queen "that you are a mortal creature," and that if she did not persevere in a godly way to the end of her life, "you cannot be blessed."[34] A furious Elizabeth had Grindal placed under house arrest. In June he was suspended from performing his functions as Archbishop for six months. In November Cecil sent him a letter asking him to make peace with the Queen, but this attempt at mediation was unsuccessful. Thereafter, Grindal was only allowed to carry out minor administrative duties. In 1580, for example, he did consecrate the bishops of Winchester and Coventry. In 1582 he was fully restored to office, but by then he was in poor health and afflicted with cataracts. Elizabeth suggested that he resign, and in fact arrangements were being made for him to do so when he died in July 1583. Effectively, there had been no active Archbishop of Canterbury for six years.

While Grindal was rendered helpless, many bishops resumed their drive against nonconformity and Presbyterianism. One of the leaders was John Aylmer, Bishop of London. Presbyterians in London wanted to take over eventual control of the official Church, and Aylmer was determined not to allow this to happen. In other parts of England where the opposition was not so entrenched, Puritans survived much better. In 1578 in Norfolk and Suffolk, for example, the Puritan gentry were able to sabotage Bishop Edmund Freke's efforts at suspending nonconformist preachers because Lord Burghley, Leicester, and Sir Francis Walsingham supported them. Between 1579 and 1583 men like Burghley perceived Catholicism as a much bigger danger than nonconformity, and were alarmed that bishops would move against Protestant preachers when they should be directing their energies against hidden Catholics.

Presbyterians tried and failed to put their agenda through the 1584 Parliament. But not only had they been unsuccessful in bringing about a change in the official policy of the church, they had another cause for concern. Upon Grindal's death, John Whitgift was appointed Archbishop of Canterbury. If Elizabeth had been upset because Grindal had been sympathetic to the Puritans, she found in Whitgift someone who shared her ideological point of view. Both were committed to the perspective that Elizabeth derived her authority in both church and state directly from God. Whitgift disliked the Cambridge Professor Cartwright, and believed that Presbyterianism was fundamentally incompatible with a monarchical state.[35] To Whitgift, they were on the same level as papists and anabaptists – they were all rebels. His immediate priority was to impose conformity on the Church. He insisted that all ministers and preachers subscribe to three articles: acknowledge royal Supremacy; agree that the Prayer Book and the Ordinal (ceremony to ordain ministers) contained nothing "contrary to the word of God"; and to accept that everything in the Thirty-Nine Articles conformed to the word of God. Some 400 ministers refused to subscribe and were suspended from their posts and refused licenses to preach. Whitgift offered the compromise that ministers would agree to use the Prayer Book, and most of the original non-subscribers signed some form of acceptance of the articles.

Elizabeth fully supported Whitgift so he did not have to be concerned that there was opposition in the Parliament and the Council. He used the Court of High Commission against Puritan ringleaders, and resisted Burghley and Leicester's attempts to protect their Presbyterian protégés. The minister George Gifford, author of *Dialogue Between a Papist and a Protestant* (1582) and *Against the Priesthood and Sacrifice of the Church of Rome* (1584), joined a group of nonconformist ministers in London and publicly refused to subscribe to the Thirty-Nine Articles. Despite appeals from Burghley and Leicester, Gifford was deprived of his living. Thomas Cartwright, recently returned to England from visiting Protestants on the Continent, was not given a license to preach. Whitgift was also working hard to reform the Church against Presbyterian charges of corruption. The Presbyterian reaction to Whitgift was equally confrontational.

Presbyterians attempted to get more of their supporters elected to the House of Commons so that religious issues could be debated in Parliament, but Elizabeth refused to allow any discussion of religion. The London-based leaders therefore decided to concentrate their energies on developing their organization and on erecting a secret Presbyterian system in the country, a shadow Church, based on the design of the Puritan divine, Walter Travers.

The late 1580s and 1590s were a hard time for the Presbyterians. Puritans were finding themselves dangerously isolated at court. In 1586 Whitgift was appointed to the Privy Council and the following year Sir

Christopher Hatton was made Lord Chancellor; both these men were strongly anti-Puritan. And Puritan supporters were dying off: Leicester in 1588, Sir Walter Mildmay in 1589, and Sir Francis Walsingham in 1590. In 1588 the Presbyterian organizer John Field died.

The 1588 spectacular defeat of the Spanish Armada also worked to weaken the base of support for the Presbyterians. It not only removed the more serious threat of Catholic invasion, though many were still concerned about further armadas in the 1590s, but more importantly, the loyalty of the English Catholics during this time of national emergency was also demonstrated. Many people also believed that if God had assisted the chosen people of England against the powerful forces arrayed against them, then there was nothing ungodly about the English Church, and no need for the reforms the Presbyterians were demanding. Many people were also upset in 1588 and 1589 by the publication of the *Marprelate Tracts*, scurrilous pamphlets that satirized the bishops.[36]

Whitgift and his associates decided the time was right for another attack on the Presbyterians. Though Cartwright and Travers were also scandalized by the *Marprelate Tracts*, their publication allowed the authorities to portray the Puritans as dangerous subversives. Sir Christopher Hatton opened the parliamentary session in 1589 with a statement that strongly defended the Church of England as it was presently constituted. Richard Bancroft, appointed a member of the High Commission in 1587, was told to arrest the Presbyterian leaders. He formulated a case against Cartwright and eight other prominent leaders. The nine were brought before the Ecclesiastical High Commission in 1590 and the Court of the Star Chamber in 1591, a court consisting of the Privy Councillors and the judges which was responsible for investigating offences against public order and perversions of justice. In the midst of the trials, two extreme Puritans, Edmund Copinger and Henry Arthington, demonstrated their outrage by publicly proclaiming William Hacket, a wandering madman, not only the returned Christ but also King.[37] Copinger and Arthington were imprisoned, and Hacket executed. While Cartwright again had no connection with Hacket, the incident was powerful propaganda against the Puritans. Cartwright and his colleagues were able to conduct their defense so effectively that the case against them could not be proved, especially since they still had some powerful friends at Court, and they were eventually released. But the trial broke their spirit, and the threat of Presbyterianism was ended for the 1590s.

John Guy argues that religious divisions were exacerbated "in a highly insidious way" in the 1590s, despite the success of Whitgift and the

Anglican bishops in breaking the Presbyterian movement and attacking the ideology of Presbyterianism. At the end of Elizabeth's reign some in London and the countryside continued to experience Puritanism spiritually with committed Puritan clergy. But many Puritan magistrates were also willing to stop attacking the Elizabethan Settlement in return for the right to consolidate their power at the local level. As a result, suggests Doran, "In this spirit, religion ceased to be a major divisive issue at both the national and the local level during the last decade of the reign."[38] Though the struggles over religion would re-emerge with severity in the seventeenth century, during her lifetime Elizabeth was the winner in her struggle to preserve the 1559 Settlement. That which had been legislated in the first year of her reign remained essentially intact as her reign ended, and England in 1603 had become a Protestant nation.

3

ENGLAND'S RELATIONS WITH OTHERS IN THE FIRST PART OF THE REIGN[1]

When Elizabeth became Queen in 1558 she not only had to deal with religion and with balancing a religious settlement that throughout her reign was poised between Catholics and Puritans, but she also had to keep England safe and independent, a balance between the two powers on the Continent, France and Spain. Elizabeth's reign was a watershed in Anglo-Continental relations. Throughout the Middle Ages France had been England's traditional enemy, and since the reign of the first Tudor king, Henry VII, Spain had been the traditional ally. By the time Elizabeth's reign ended, England was the uneasy ally of France and the enemy of, and at war with, Spain. England's dealings with both these countries were further complicated by its relations within the British Isles with Scotland, made even more difficult because of Elizabeth's cousin Mary Stuart, and with Ireland, which England was determined to control at all costs, no matter how brutal and expensive such an undertaking might be. One of England's main strategic goals was to prevent foreign interference in both Scotland and Ireland, perceived as the gates to England.[2]

Just as there was a major shift in England's relations with France and Spain during Elizabeth's reign, so too was there a transformation in Anglo-Scottish relations. When Elizabeth became Queen, England and Scotland were at war; by 1603 Scotland's King James VI peacefully succeeded Elizabeth as King of England too, and in the intervening years England and Scotland had eventually developed a diplomatic relation as two

Protestant kingdoms.[3] The policy of repression and colonization in Ireland under Elizabeth, however, encouraged bitter divisiveness that has lasted for centuries.

Foreign policy was traditionally in the preserve of the monarch, but it was even more important for Elizabeth to have some control over it because for the first 20 to 25 years of her reign, the question of England's foreign policy was so inextricably connected with the question of her marriage. Historians debate about how much Elizabeth really directed foreign policy. R. B. Wernham is convinced that Elizabeth did not simply drift and respond to external events, that she did have a coherent foreign policy, one that she herself set. He argues that we can see it in her dealings with the Netherlands, where from 1567 she pursued a number of goals: expelling the Spanish army from the Netherlands; preventing the French from gaining power in the Netherlands; and seeing the Netherlanders themselves, under continued Spanish protection, restored to their ancient liberties and measure of home rule they had enjoyed under Charles V. Wernham also gives the example of Elizabeth's long-standing preference for an understanding with the French royal government instead of thorough support for the Huguenots. Elizabeth also demonstrated a consistent appreciation of the danger from the revived sea-power of Spain in the 1590s. While the conception and initiation of policy was frequently left to the royal councillors, Elizabeth would either accept, reject, or modify what they suggested. Wallace MacCaffrey also argues that the final decision on foreign policy was Elizabeth's.[4] It is certainly the case that the final decision was Elizabeth's when it came to the decision of marrying, or, as it turned out, not marrying, her various suitors. D. M. Loades, however, describes Elizabeth's foreign policy, like that in the reign of Edward VI, as "reactive rather than proactive."[5]

Most of the work dealing with foreign policy was done by and through the Principal Secretary, who conducted the routine correspondence and drafted letters for Elizabeth to send in response. Early in her reign Cecil occasionally attempted to keep key information from Elizabeth, and was upset when she received news directly that did not first pass under his control and scrutiny. Elizabeth, however, kept a close watch over the Secretary's work, and she expected her ambassadors and agents, military and naval commanders to write to her directly about serious matters.

The Principal Secretary obviously had considerable influence in the shaping and carrying out of foreign policy.[6] This was especially the case in the first decade and a half of the reign, when Cecil was Principal

Secretary. Elizabeth preferred to have state papers read to her, and Cecil, suggests Wernham, "not infrequently found himself acting as a sort of verbal reader's digest." But historians have also found significant evidence in the documents that Elizabeth was watching foreign policy issues with a great deal of care.[7] Part of the reason for Cecil's influence was Elizabeth's trust in him, and the position of the Secretary had less influence between 1573 and 1590 when it was held by Sir Francis Walsingham, with brief assistance from, in turn, Sir Thomas Smith, Thomas Wilson, and William Davison, the last for only a very brief and unhappy moment. Though Cecil, now Lord Burghley, held the office of Lord Treasurer, Elizabeth continued to consult with him on matters of foreign as well as domestic policy, and most English ambassadors and agents, naval and military commanders, continued to correspond with him as well as with Mr Secretary Walsingham. Walsingham, however, was also of great importance to Elizabeth's government, especially in the area of spying and intelligence.

Intricately connected to foreign policy issues was the question of the Queen's marriage. Most of the people around Elizabeth very much wanted her to marry, though not everyone shared this perspective. Sir Thomas Smith thought that given the dangers of childbirth, Elizabeth was safer if she stayed a spinster, stating that "every hour" women were "sent from their childbed to their burial."[8] Smith's position, though reasonable, was unusual. As her reign progressed, Elizabeth faced more and more pressure from her Council and from Parliament, whenever she called them. But this pressure was not the only reason for the various courtships. Even though Elizabeth claimed to dislike the idea of marriage, and prefer the single state, she also encouraged the negotiations. She loved being courted, was "greedy for marriage proposals," as Sir Henry Sidney put it. Elizabeth well understood the political importance of her marriage, and how useful it would be as a negotiating tool in her relations with her powerful neighbors. Jones describes it as a "brilliant diplomatic policy," though at times it left her subjects utterly frustrated, and wondering if she really cared about their welfare.[9]

Though Elizabeth engaged in many marriage negotiations, it is difficult to know how serious she was about actually marrying. Haigh suggests that certainly by 1576, but perhaps as early as 1563, though marriage had become for Elizabeth, "her chosen weapon in diplomatic intrigue," she had no intention of actually marrying; rather she kept the marriage issue open as a political weapon, "to entice suitors and to tame claimants to the throne." But Wallace MacCaffrey argues that while Elizabeth had a basic antipathy toward marriage, in 1566 "she had to face the fact that marriage might become an unavoidable political imperative."[10]

Susan Doran, however, argues that Elizabeth truly wanted to marry on two occasions during her reign: in the fall of 1560, after the death of Robert Dudley's wife Amy, she seriously contemplated marrying her favorite, and in 1579 she again demonstrated a strong desire to marry Francis, Duke of Anjou (formerly Alençon). She was also willing to consider marriage with the Archduke Charles of Austria in the mid-1560s and with Henry Duke of Anjou in 1570–71 because she was under such pressure from her councillors and Parliaments. Doran argues that to understand why these various negotiations failed, historians need to concentrate not on Elizabeth's character, but instead on the debates that surrounded these courtships, and the political strategies of the opponents of each one. Both with Dudley in 1560 and in the Anjou courtship in 1579, Doran is convinced Elizabeth really wanted to marry, but that the active opposition of some leading men in her Council convinced her that it would be politically unwise and potentially even disastrous to proceed. In each case there was enough opposition and political intrigue to make the marriage, even though Elizabeth was willing, too politically dangerous for her.[11] Yet if one looks deeply into Elizabeth's psyche, one wonders if she would have ever been willing to marry, whatever the political situation.[12]

In 1558 Elizabeth became Queen in the midst of England's involvement in a war between Spain and France.[13] England's entanglement in the war came out of Mary's marriage to Philip of Spain, and joining Spain against France was of no strategic value to England; rather, in January 1558 it resulted in the loss of Calais, the last remnant of England's medieval French empire. Though people in England were distraught, the loss in Calais had more to do with honor and symbolism than any reality.[14] The first few months of Elizabeth's reign were spent preparing to defend England from a possible invasion of the French or their allies, the Scots. Mary of Guise, the mother of the young Queen of Scotland, Mary Stuart, was Regent of Scotland; Mary herself, resident in the French royal household since she was six, had married the dauphin, Francis, in April 1558. After Mary I's death in November, rumors abounded that the French would push Mary Stuart's claims to the English throne, since Catholics viewed Elizabeth as an illegitimate heretic and thus ineligible to rule.

Elizabeth, though Calais was lost, did gain something from the peace negotiations with France and the April 1559 Treaty of Cateau-Cambrésis was something of a triumph for Elizabeth. Though England did not salvage much from the war, in a face-saving gesture the French agreed to hold Calais for eight years and then either return it or pay an indemnity.[15] More importantly, in the treaty the French King Henry II abandoned the claim of his daughter-in-law Mary Stuart and recognized Elizabeth as lawful Queen of England.[16] The Treaty of Cateau-Cambrésis freed Elizabeth and England from a foreign policy disaster, and allowed her to start considering other ways of shaping policy to keep England safe and secure. Yet even with the treaty, Elizabeth and her advisors were still concerned about French intervention in Scotland and Ireland.

In the early 1560s Elizabeth was much more hostile to France than she was to Spain, and wanted to end French domination in Scotland. When Mary had arrived in France as a child in August 1548, Henry II had proclaimed that France and Scotland were now one country, a point of view that gravely distressed the English. Henry had signed the treaty, but the situation became more urgent after he was accidentally killed in a tournament in July 1559. When Mary Stuart and Francis II briefly became King and Queen of France, Mary included the arms of England in the coat of arms on the French royal hangings and the plate, and on a Scottish Great Seal that they used.[17] Cecil did all he could to bring this to Elizabeth's attention, recognizing how furious this would make her. At the same time in 1559, a Protestant and nationalist revolt in Scotland had begun when the Queen Regent declared Protestant ministers outlaws. The rebels, known as the Lords of the Congregation, wanted Catholicism abolished. Instead, the Queen Regent responded by sending for more French troops. Elizabeth at first secretly, then openly with arms, supported the rebels. The French, having much to deal with at home and lacking support in Scotland after the death of the Queen Regent, Mary of Guise, in July 1560, agreed to a withdrawal from Scotland. The Treaty of Edinburgh of July 1560, which stated that Mary and Francis would give up their claim to the English throne and withdraw their troops from Scotland, was not ratified by Mary, but the French forces departed in mid-July except for a token handful. The English also agreed to withdraw their troops, though their alliance with the Scottish Protestant nobles continued. Though this may have had more to do with Elizabeth's parsimony that anything else, the Scottish were greatly relieved by this, and by Cecil's awareness of Scottish sensibilities during the negotiations.[18] Wernham suggests that while the original support for this plan was all Cecil's, "for the skillfulness of its timing the Queen herself was largely responsible." MacCaffrey, on the other hand, considers

Elizabeth to be a more reluctant mover in this enterprise. Certainly, as Hiram Morgan points out, one of the consistent themes of Cecil's foreign policy in the early part of Elizabeth's reign was to create a British Isles that was both united and Protestant.[19] Though the Scottish Parliament promulgated a Protestant confession of faith in August, without the assent of Mary it was not binding, and the struggle between Protestant and Catholics in Scotland would continue. Francis's death of a brain tumor in December 1560 ended Mary's career as Queen of France and began it as Queen of Scotland.

If intervention in Scotland was successful, armed intervention on behalf of the Huguenots in France, a policy strongly encouraged by Robert Dudley, was a disaster. Elizabeth alienated her Protestant allies by attempting to negotiate the return of Calais as the price for her aid, and when in March 1563 the Regent and Queen Mother Catherine de Medici agreed to a truce with the Huguenots, they turned on the English because of the demand for Calais. Many of the Englishmen in France under the command of Robert's brother Ambrose, Earl of Warwick, died, mostly from the plague. Elizabeth learned this lesson well: she could not depend on the reliability of foreign Protestant allies, especially when her own concerns were for England. She was extremely reluctant to intervene on behalf of Protestants in other countries again.

Relations, while still not strongly hostile, were also growing more difficult with Spain in the early 1560s. The Calvinist minority in the Netherlands was becoming stronger, and both Cardinal Granvelle, Philip's chief minister there, and the Regent Margaret of Parma were worried that English merchants at Bruges and Antwerp were providing the Calvinists with aid. Philip perceived the possibility of an international Protestant conspiracy with England playing a leading role. The English pirates who were attacking Catholic merchant ships encouraged this perspective. Granvelle was also upset that the English had considerably increased customs duties.

Towards the end of 1563 Granvelle found the opportunity to express his hostility to England. English troops, returning home from the disaster in France, brought with them the plague. Granvelle used the plague as his rationale for placing an embargo on all cloth imports from London. Elizabeth retaliated, and trade between England and the Netherlands crashed to a halt. For England, customs duties were critical to the financial health of the country. Along with land revenues, they were the main source of regular income. As much as one-half of the cloth that was produced in England was exported. A slow-down or stoppage in exports not only had impact on the spinners, weavers, and others who produced the cloth, but also on sheep farmers and landowners.

In 1564 the English government negotiated an agreement with Emden and the Merchant Adventurers transferred their trade there from Antwerp. It was not really a satisfactory solution, however, and the English continued to negotiate with Spain. Granvelle was dismissed and in December they reached a settlement. When trade reopened in January 1565, the Merchant Adventurers flocked back to Antwerp. The brief shutting down of trade caused great concern in England. There was a widespread belief that England needed Spanish friendship as a balance to France, and that an important aspect of that friendship was the Antwerp trade. During the next few years, however, mounting opposition to Spanish rule in the Netherlands and anti-Catholic sentiment at home, cast more and more doubts upon Antwerp's adequacy as an international trading center. In May 1567 the English came to an agreement with Hamburg.

Only a few months later, in August 1567, the Duke of Alva marched into Brussels at the head of 10 000 Spanish troops to stamp out the rebellion in the Netherlands. He was soon reinforced by Italian, German, and Walloon levies of over 50 000 men. Suddenly, there was this large, strategically placed army. Wernham perceives this as one of the great turning points of early modern history. "The Netherlands westward frontier lay a bare ninety miles from Paris; its westward coast lay little more than thirty miles from the coast of Kent, little more than a hundred miles from the Thames estuary and London. For both France and England, therefore, the presence of this great Spanish army, this shifting northward of the center of gravity of Spanish military power, was a matter of urgent concern."[20] This concern would have great impact for England in many of its dealings.

At the same time that Elizabeth was involved in French, Scottish, and Dutch affairs, she was also considering marriage proposals from a number of foreign courts. At the very beginning of her reign, she quickly rejected the proposal from her former brother-in-law Philip. She expressed little interest in Erik of Sweden, despite his determined courtship, and the enthusiasm of some of her subjects over having a Protestant king as her husband. Elizabeth in 1559–60 also did not take seriously the candidacy of the Austrian Archduke Charles. Despite all of the Spanish ambassador Bishop de Quadra's attempts to encourage the marriage, Elizabeth confided she would not marry Charles as she had "no wish to give up solitude and our lonely life." No one really believed Elizabeth meant this seriously, but at the beginning of her reign many people believed the best match for the Queen would be an Englishman.

By the mid-1560s the situation had changed. The only strong English candidate was Robert Dudley, and there was far too much antipathy to the match for Elizabeth to marry him. Though she appears to have briefly considered it, the response of her Council and the people convinced her it was impossible. There were a number of obstacles in the marriage negotiations in the 1560s of Elizabeth to the Archduke Charles; however, there were also ways in which the match was attractive to the English. In 1563 Elizabeth's government let the Emperor Ferdinand know they would be interested in negotiating a marriage with his younger son.[21]

In the mid-1560s the English people were acutely concerned over the possibility of a disputed succession. In 1563 Mary Stuart, the widowed Catholic Queen of Scotland, was attempting to negotiate an advantageous marriage that would give Spain or France a presence in Scotland that could be used as a base to move against the English. Elizabeth's extreme concern over who might be Mary Stuart's second husband perhaps contributed to her need to consider marriage herself. There was talk of a Spanish marriage, possibly with Philip's heir Don Carlos, or a French match with her brother-in-law Charles IX, younger brother of her first husband Francis II. Mary even listened to Elizabeth's incredible proposal that she marry Robert Dudley if this meant that she would be formally named the heir of England.

None of these proposals came to anything, and in the summer of 1565 Mary married her Catholic cousin Henry Stuart, Lord Darnley. Even though Elizabeth herself had narrowed Mary's choices for marriage partners, this marriage frightened Elizabeth and her Council. The marriage with Darnley could be seen as strengthening Mary's claim to the English throne since he was also a claimant through their common grandmother, Margaret Tudor, Henry VIII's older sister. Soon after the Darnley marriage, Mary increased the anxieties for the English by discussions with Shane O'Neill, who was leading an insurrection in Ireland and defining himself as a defender of the Catholic faith.[22]

The English saw a marriage alliance with the Archduke as a way to restore the balance of power lost with Mary's marriage. There was no other suitor who had the requisite status. Elizabeth might well have also seen the negotiations as a way of moderating some of the ill will that had begun to develop between England and Spain, to increase good will between England and the Hapsburgs.

A large problem in the negotiation for the English was Archduke Charles's Catholicism. Elizabeth placed another obstacle in the way of the negotiations as well: she said that she would not sign any marriage contract unless she had first seen the Archduke. The Emperor's negotiators claimed that Charles would lose his dignity were he to come to England prior to a formal betrothal, on approval as it were, but without his coming to England first, Elizabeth stated that a formal betrothal was impossible. Elizabeth's stand both kept her from having a spouse whom she did not find attractive or was not appreciative enough of her charms; and, however, it also meant that she had more control over just how serious a number of marriage negotiations would become.

The English reopened the marriage negotiations in 1563; by 1565 the new Emperor Maximillian, son of Ferdinand, had sent an Imperial envoy, Baron von Mitterburg, to London and most of the Privy Council encouraged the marriage. The strongest supporters were the Duke of Norfolk, and the Earl of Sussex. For a number of councillors, the fear of a disputed succession was so strong that the concern over Charles's Catholicism receded. They optimistically believed that the Hapsburgs were more flexible about religious practice than was indeed the case. Cecil, despite his commitment to the Anglican Settlement, argued for the marriage in the hope that Charles would eventually agree to total conformity. Sussex realized this was unrealistic, but he believed that the negotiators could reach a compromise: Charles would privately go to mass but he would also attend Anglican services with Elizabeth.

Charles's practice of Catholicism was not the only issue to be resolved. There was also disagreement about who should pay the costs of Charles's household in England and what would be Charles's title and role in the governing of England. These might have been resolved, but Elizabeth rejected the idea of Charles attending Catholic services in England. By the end of August the imperial ambassador had informed Charles's brother the Emperor that the negotiations were at an impasse. The marriage would not happen unless the English were willing to change their stand.

But whether or not Elizabeth intended seriously to consider marrying Charles, she did not want the negotiations to end. In May 1566 she sent Thomas Danett to Emperor Maximilian to ask him to reconsider his position on the open practice of Charles's religion. Elizabeth hoped that continuing the negotiations would ease the pressure at home, especially with the 1566 Parliament, which did discuss the succession, but could agree neither on a potential husband for Elizabeth nor a designated heir.

As well as dealing with pressure at home, Elizabeth may have also thought that continuing the negotiations was a way to keep Philip II's good will, at least for a while longer. Maximilian was as adamant about religion as Elizabeth and refused to allow the marriage without the open practice of Catholicism for Charles. Yet Norfolk, Sussex, and Cecil continued to encourage Elizabeth to marry Charles. With pressure from both Parliament and her Privy Council, Elizabeth agreed to send Sussex to Austria to continue the negotiations. But Elizabeth kept finding reasons to postpone his departure, and many people had more and more doubts there would ever be a marriage between Elizabeth and Charles.[23]

Finally, Elizabeth gave permission to Sussex to depart, and he arrived in Vienna in early August. Sussex worked hard and took his job seriously; eventually he and Maximilian agreed on a solution: Charles would privately worship as he wished if he would also publicly attend Anglican services with the Queen. There were certainly still some differences in interpretation over what this settlement entailed, but Sussex believed the crucial issue had been worked out and the marriage could go forward. Elizabeth, however, then backpedalled, and said that she could not make a commitment without discussing it with the Council.[24] And her Council was split on the decision. Leicester led the opposition, which also included Pembroke, Clinton, Howard of Effingham, and a close Leicester ally, Sir James Croft. Unfortunately, the ranks were thinner for the supporters of the marriage. While Cecil was still a strong supporter, Sussex was of course still in Vienna, and their other committed ally, the Duke of Norfolk, had been absent from Court for several months; the death of his wife in childbirth had left him depressed and ill. Though Sussex wrote to Norfolk begging him to attend, Norfolk felt too ill to obey Elizabeth's summons to attend the Council meeting that was convened to discuss the marriage, and would only write to the Queen that he favored the marriage.

Those who were opposed to the marriage with the Archduke presented the case that a foreign Catholic husband would cause religious and political unrest. The marriage would also encourage English Catholics to practice their religion as well, and create great animosities in the most zealous Protestants. For those in favor of the marriage, there was even more grave danger to the realm if an unmarried Elizabeth were to die causing a disputed succession and threat of civil war. Elizabeth listened to the discussion and came to the conclusion that Charles should not come to England even for a visit; there was no point since she would refuse to allow Charles to celebrate the mass even in private. Elizabeth wrote to

inform Sussex, and all hope for the marriage ended. Sussex was furious
with Leicester for blocking the marriage for what he considered selfish,
political motives. While Susan Doran argues that though Elizabeth
ended the negotiations, she engaged in them in good faith, but would
not marry anyone who did not practice her religion. Doran's perspective
modifies MacCaffrey's belief that "she was probably not entirely insin-
cere when she expressed her willingness to marry for the sake of her
realm. But in her own mind this eventuality remained a remote –
indeed, almost an abstract – possibility."[25]

By the beginning of 1568 the marriage negotiations with the Archduke
had finally ground to a halt. The Duke of Alva was established in the
Netherlands with his army, and tension was growing in the relations
between England and Spain. Early in the year Philip had written to his
ambassador, Guzman de Silva, conveying his friendship and kind feelings to Elizabeth. But that spring Philip II expelled the resident English
ambassador Dr John Mann (or Man) to enforced residence in a village
outside Madrid and let him know he would no longer be received at
court. Mann had been resident in Spain since 1565, but he was not the
best choice for the position. As a Protestant cleric, he made his contempt
for Catholics all too apparent. De Silva was able to calm the situation and
Elizabeth agreed to recall Dr Mann. But the English began to see Mann's
expulsion as a bad portent that summer, as Alva was doing all he could to
crush the Protestant resistance in the Netherlands. Despite the concern
over Alva, when William of Orange attempted in the summer of 1568 to
raise a revolt and drive Alva out, the English made no effort to help.
Elizabeth and her Council did not want war with Spain. Just at a time
when careful diplomacy was most important, in September Philip acceded
to de Silva's request for a transfer and replaced him with Guerau
DeSpes, a friend of the Duke of Feria and the English Catholic exiles.
Instead of an urbane, sophisticated man of good judgment who had won
the friendship of Elizabeth and the respect of Cecil, the ambassador was
now a man ready to stir up controversy and who saw the Protestants as
the enemy.

The problems in the Netherlands continued to have impact on England. Alva was able to defeat William, but it cost much more than Philip
had wanted to spend. The only way Alva could keep control of his army
was to pay them. Philip had hoped the Netherlands would provide
him with some needed wealth, but instead of being able to send funds
back to Philip, Alva had to ask for more. And Philip was burdened with
costly expenditures throughout his empire. He had a serious rebellion

of the Moriscos in Spain and a growing Turkish threat to the Western Mediterranean. Philip decided to obtain the money he needed for Alva by borrowing £80 000 from the bankers of Genoa. The money was sent to Alva on five small ships, but bad weather and Huguenot privateers forced the ships to take shelter in Plymouth and Southampton in late November.

Originally, Elizabeth assured DeSpes that she would send the money on to Alva. Then Cecil discovered that legally the money still belonged to the Genoese bankers until it was handed over at Antwerp, and that quite possibly they might be willing to lend it to the English Queen instead. As soon as he heard this was a possibility, DeSpes became so upset that he immediately urged Alva to order the counter-seizure of English ships and goods in the Netherlands and advise Philip to do the same in Spain. This was before he knew that Elizabeth had definitely determined to take over the loan, which she did in fact do. Alva carried out the seizure, and when news of this reached London on 3 January 1569 Elizabeth immediately retaliated in kind; the government ordered the seizure of all Flemish and Spanish property and placed DeSpes under house arrest.

Alva refused to be overwhelmed by these events. He realized he had been pushed prematurely into this action by DeSpes and sent an envoy to England. Elizabeth and Cecil dragged out the negotiations. They refused to cede anything on the matter of the treasure, but Elizabeth also made it clear that she did not want to go to war and the crisis was smoothed over. Some Protestants might view this as a brave stroke to embarrass their enemies, but the quarrel between England and Spain was also difficult for Elizabeth and Cecil. Plenty of merchants and nobles in 1569 believed that Spain's friendship was essential for both England's safety and the smooth continuation of the Antwerp trade. A strong anti-Cecil movement received more ammunition.

Relations between England and Spain were also shifting in 1568–69 because of dramatic changes in Scotland. While Mary Stuart's marriage to Darnley provided her with an heir, the future James VI of Scotland and I of England, it was otherwise a disaster. Lord Darnley was arrogant and incompetent, drunken and probably diseased. By participating in the murder of her Italian secretary, David Rizzio, he had alienated his wife, and when he returned to her side and turned against his fellow conspirators, he alienated everyone else as well. Yet his murder in February 1567 was startling news, and people were even more shocked when, only a few months later on 15 May, Mary married James Hepburn, Earl of Bothwell, the man all Scotland was calling Darnley's murderer.

Mary insisted that Bothwell had raped her, so that marriage to him was the only way to save her honor – a claim most people found disingenuous at best. Scotland rose in rebellion; Bothwell managed to escape to Denmark, where he would later die insane in a Danish prison, but Mary was captured and returned to Edinburgh where the crowds chanted "burn the whore." Elizabeth did all she could to try to have Mary restored to nominal sovereignty, which, as MacCaffrey suggests, says more for her decency than for her political sense in this case.[26] The Scottish lords refused, however, and Mary was forced to abdicate in favor of her infant son, with her Protestant half-brother the Earl of Moray as Regent. Mary was imprisoned, but in May 1568 she managed to escape. After yet another unsuccessful rising in her name, she escaped to England, where she was to stay for 19 years until her execution.[27] Moray did not want Mary back in Scotland. In July 1569 he held a convention at Perth where the lords voted against any restoration for Mary and, for good measure, declared it treason to uphold her claim. But Mary proved an unquiet guest in England as well. Soon after she arrived in England she sent word to DeSpes that if his master would help her, she would be Queen of England and in six months mass would be said all over the country. For nearly the next two decades, Philip of Spain had to consider his willingness to assist Mary Stuart's ambitions for the English throne: was a Catholic Queen with French connections better or worse for Spain than Protestant Elizabeth?

Another issue Philip had to consider was whether or not to give aid to his co-religionists in Ireland. Elizabeth had inherited an extremely problematic situation in Ireland, and the English administration in Ireland had virtually no control over the lands outside the boundaries of the Pale. One of the major shifts in dealing with Ireland in the early Elizabethan period was the alienation of a previously loyal Pale community from the English government in Ireland, and a greater potential for foreign intervention which led to the expanding English presence in Ireland.[28] As the Pale community was faced with unprecedented rates of taxation and deprived of the traditional benefits of office, they became increasingly disillusioned with the Dublin government and began to slowly disassociate themselves from the cause of what the English called Irish reform. They began to display contempt for the "New English" administrators and distinguished themselves by calling themselves "the Old English". Another way they distanced themselves from the English and established their own identity was the commitment to Catholicism. The situation in Ireland became even more difficult as Elizabeth's reign progressed. Insurrections, or as the English would term them, rebellions, led by the Irish to expel the English were not only expensive to suppress, but also extremely violent and bloody, leading to even more ill-will.[29] Eventually, some English observers in Ireland, including Edmund Spenser, came to believe that reform was a miserable failure and it was impossible to ever achieve a rule of law in Ireland. William Palmer argues that, as a result, many in England believed the only solution was the immediate and complete forcible destruction of Irish culture.[30]

If the Netherlands were a matter in which Philip hated interference, and what many Catholics viewed as an international Protestant conspiracy, the mirror image of this was Ireland, which Protestant England was attempting to dominate. Early in the reign English Protestants feared that if they did not control Ireland, it would be a place that Catholic France or Spain could use to invade England. This view certainly dominated the relations early in the reign with Scotland as well. In 1561 Christopher Hatton described both as "a postern gate through which those bent on the destruction of the country might enter."[31] Palmer suggests that "The Netherlands was to Spain what Ireland was to England, a troublesome, but strategic territory which had to be kept under control."[32] Just as Philip perceived the Calvinists in the Netherlands as monstrous, so too did the English view the Catholics in Ireland; as Hiram Morgan points out, the rhetoric of the Irish, particularly that of Hugh O'Neill at the end of the century, was a mirror image of the patriotic language of the Dutch rebels.[33] In truth, the English had little to fear from the Irish lords. But if the Irish lords were supported by French, Spanish, papal, or Scottish assistance, they could pose a formidable threat. Palmer is convinced that at the same time military commitment and levels of taxation rose in the 1560s, there was also an increasing fear of, and the actuality of, foreign intrigue in Ireland. At the beginning of the reign the English had to deal with the rebellion of Shane O'Neill, who had been furious that Mary's government had conferred the earldom of Tyrone on his illegitimate half-brother Matthew, whom Shane later had murdered. O'Neill was negotiating with both Charles IX and Mary Stuart for military aid, and Elizabeth told her Lord Deputy, Sir Henry Sidney, to do whatever he needed to. Sidney marched against O'Neill in the winter of 1566–67, waging a successful campaign against him. Though it was his Gaelic and Scottish enemies in Ireland who in the end killed O'Neill, Sidney's campaign had convinced the Scottish settlers, the Macdonalds and the O'Donnells, that royal power was superior to Shane O'Neill. Though O'Neill was dead, Henry Sidney was still aware of the possibility of foreign intervention. As early as 1567, Henry Sidney told Elizabeth that it would be easy for Philip to take over Munster and Connacht; he wanted her to perceive the need of greater security on the south coast of Ireland.[34]

Sidney's attempt to re-establish English authority over Ireland in the 1560s generated dreams of conquest and colonization. Sidney's scheme was to bring all of Ireland under English control through colonization. He allowed a number of English adventurers to seize land, even land of Irish people who were loyal or had made their submission to Elizabeth. Such action convinced Irish lords that the English colonizers would appropriate any land they wanted, and no one was safe. A group of lords in Munster chose James Fitzmaurice Fitzgerald to lead a rebellion. In what was in part a self-fulfilling prophecy, Fitzmaurice sought aid from Philip II.[35] In 1569 Sir Humphrey Gilbert and Nicholas Malby were able to suppress, though not completely put down, the Fitzmaurice rebellion. After the Northern rebellion was ended in England in 1570, two of the northern rebels went to Ireland to join the Fitzmaurice rebellion as it continued. Some members of Elizabeth's government, particularly Sir Francis Walsingham, became convinced that a compliant Ireland was crucial to England's security. Henry Sidney was recalled from Ireland in 1571 and the Fitzmaurice rebellion subdued by the new deputy, Sir William Fitzwilliam, and Sir John Perrot, the lord president of Munster. Fitzmaurice submitted in 1573 and fled to the Continent two years later, where he worried the English by his attempts to obtain aid from Spain, France, Portugal, or the Pope.

The situation with Spain, and anxieties over Ireland and the Netherlands were such that the English believed it was in their self-interest to work out some alliance with the French. In 1571 Sir Francis Walsingham went to Paris to negotiate the possible marriage of Elizabeth with Henry, the Duke of Anjou, younger brother of Charles IX. Elizabeth did all she could to convince Catherine de Medici and her son that she was serious, but whether she would have had any intention of actually going through with such a marriage is another issue. While Anjou's Catholicism, and his refusal to compromise on the question of his worship, stalled the negotiations with France as these issues had earlier with the Empire, Walsingham was able to use the possibility of the marriage to try to encourage better relations with France, and the negotiations ended with short-term agreements between the two countries.

The Ridolfi Plot to put Mary Stuart and the Duke of Norfolk on the throne with the support of troops from the Netherlands in the fall of

1571 made the need of an agreement with France all the more necessary. The French also found a Spanish army in the Netherlands disturbing to their security. The French Huguenots, however, were also extremely concerned about their situation in France unless there was a strong treaty with the English. By the next April the two countries had signed the Treaty of Blois, a defensive treaty against Spain where France also promised to stay out of the affairs of Mary Stuart and Scotland.[36]

Once both sides had signed the agreement, the English negotiators in Paris were relieved not only for England, but because they were convinced this would give the Huguenots more security. Walsingham, still in Paris, looked forward to the marriage of the Protestant cousin Henry of Navarre to Catherine's daughter, Margaret. But Catherine, caught in a struggle between the ultra-Catholics led by the Guise family and the Huguenots, was concerned that she and her son were too much under the influence of the leading Huguenot of France, Admiral Gaspard de Coligny, and many scholars believe that she arranged to have him assassinated. The assassination attempt failed, and on St Bartholomew's Day, August 24, 1572, Catherine, to hide her role in the assassination attempt, ordered the slaughter of thousands of Protestants. The streets in Paris ran red and the violence soon spread to the countryside. Walsingham did all he could to protect the English Protestants who sheltered at his residence; none of the English who experienced the massacre ever forgot it. Catherine and her son's confused and contradictory explanation did nothing to stem the English horror; though the treaty was not abrogated, English people were appalled at the idea of Elizabeth marrying into the French royal house or developing a closer alliance.

Many English Protestants were still appalled half a dozen years later when the idea of marriage to a son of the French royal house was again discussed. Her erstwhile suitor Anjou had become Henry III in 1574 upon the death of Charles IX and the marriage partner being offered was his younger brother Francis, once Duke of Alençon, now Duke of Anjou.[37] The political motivation for this negotiation was to gain support for anti-Spanish forces in the Netherlands. The English government was committed to the view that the Spanish had to be kept from imposing absolute rule there, but they were also uneasy with French involvement over which they had no control. Unlike some of her more vehemently Protestant advisors, such as Walsingham, Elizabeth had not supported an independent Netherlands. Elizabeth was afraid that an independent Netherlands would soon be controlled by the French and this would be no better for English security. She did, however, want to see the Dutch restored to their ancient liberties, to the semi-independent status that they had earlier in the century under Philip's father, Charles V. Elizabeth did not, as the Earl of Sussex put it, want the Spanish to tyrannize the Netherlands but equally she did not want the French to save them at the cost of possessing them. If Elizabeth were to marry Anjou, she could keep the French under control and pressure the Spanish to come to a reasonable settlement with the insurgents in the Netherlands.[38]

Elizabeth also, however, seems to have shown far more personal interest in this potential marriage than in previous ones: she agreed that the French Prince might privately practice his Catholicism, she had him visit twice during the negotiations (August 1579 and November 1581) and even publicly stated that she would marry him. But Elizabeth found many of the English were strongly opposed to the marriage. The massacre was still a vivid memory. Sir Philip Sidney sent Elizabeth an open letter against the marriage, calling Anjou "the son of the Jezebel of our age."[39] But it was not only that Anjou was French. After years of begging Elizabeth to marry, a number of English people were concerned that she was now too old and the prospect of childbirth too dangerous.

John Stubbs, trained as a lawyer with Puritan leanings, believed he was expressing his great love and loyalty to his sovereign in his pamphlet, *The Discoverie of a Gaping Gulf whereinto England is like to be swallowed* (1579) which argued forcibly against the proposed marriage. Stubbs was distressed by the idea of a French Catholic husband who might dominate Elizabeth, and worried that Elizabeth was too old to safely have a child. He even suggested that Anjou's true motivation was the expectation that Elizabeth would die in childbirth so that the French could then take over the country. Elizabeth was infuriated by the pamphlet's argument and had Stubbs tried for seditious libel. Found guilty, the punishment was the severing of his right hand. The crowd watched this brutality in sullen silence; only Stubbs himself cried "God save the Queen" before he fainted.

Elizabeth's Privy Council, which met in October 1579, was also strongly opposed to the match. Its only supporters were Burghley and Sussex. This response upset Elizabeth, who told them she had expected them to support the marriage as the best means to safety for her and the realm. In November she informed her Council that she had decided to marry and did not want to hear any more objections; rather, they should consider what steps were necessary so that she could accomplish her purpose. But the agitation was so intense that in January, Elizabeth wrote to Anjou that she could not go forward. Henry III, however, wanted the marriage as the price for an alliance. MacCaffrey argues that while Elizabeth could have made the marriage with Anjou, it would have been "at the cost of rupturing the amity which bound together the inner world of the Elizabethan Court and which by extension ensured stability to the whole English political order."[40]

In October 1581 Anjou returned to England. He wanted more English support against the Spanish in the Low Countries. He also still hoped that he could convince Elizabeth to agree to the marriage. On November 22 Elizabeth surprised Anjou and her Court by promising to marry the French Prince. Yet even this public declaration in the end was meaningless. By February she had lent Anjou £70 000 and sent him back to the Low Countries, where the war continued badly. Elizabeth had given Anjou some support, but had signed no treaty nor promised him troops. He had returned to France before his death in 1584, leaving the situation in the Netherlands perilous. The English were by now in an uneasy alliance against the Spanish, but everyone recognized that it would not be sealed by a royal marriage. Many of the English did not want a close alliance with the French because of their horror over the slaughter of the Huguenots.

Yet, at the same time, there was a new and much more serious attempt to colonize Ireland that also had elements of a massacre. The expedition led by Walter Devereaux, Earl of Essex, in 1573 amounted to a national undertaking. Elizabeth instructed Essex to avoid molesting the Gaelic inhabitants and instead to devote his energies to destroying the Scottish settlement in Ulster. But Essex soon became frustrated by the Gaelic chiefs, even those who had professed their loyalty. In December 1574 Essex seized Sir Brian MacPhelim O'Neill, his wife, and some of his kinsmen at a Christmas feast. Two hundred of O'Neill's followers were massacred on the spot, and O'Neill and his wife were later executed in Dublin. Essex's violence only escalated. The next year he led an attack on Rathlin Island; he and his men slaughtered 600 inhabitants. One of his followers, Edward Barkley, described later, "how godly a deed it is to overthrow so wicked a race the world may judge; for my part I think there cannot be a greater sacrifice to God." Elizabeth herself praised Essex for the service he did in bringing that "rude and barbarous nation to civility ... and to oppose yourself and your forces to them whom reason and duty cannot bridle." Sir Humphrey Gilbert was equally violent in Munster. He virtually declared war on every man, woman, and child there, wanting to create such fear in the Irish that they would submit. He ordered his men to behead the Irish rebels and then place the heads on each side of the path leading to his tent; all the prisoners had to pass through the lane of heads. Thomas Churchyard, who accompanied Gilbert, justified the unjustifiable in a pamphlet with the reason that "through the terror which the people conceived thereby it made short wars."[41]

Nicholas Canny argues that Englishmen such as Essex and Gilbert believed that "they were absolved from normal ethical restraints" when they dealt with the native population of Ireland.[42] This echoed some of the religious violence in France, and was a dreadful doubling/mirroring of the Spanish treatment in the Netherlands, and for both, the fear of international religious conspiracies and plotting seemed to allow for this horrific behavior.[43] In the first two decades of Elizabeth's reign, England had been briefly involved militarily in Scotland and France, and much more substantially in Ireland. As the reign continued, problems in both Ireland and the Netherlands were to worsen, and conflict with Spain loomed larger and larger over the English landscape.

4

ENGLAND'S RELATIONS WITH OTHERS IN THE LAST PART OF THE REIGN[1]

The mid-1580s were a time of crisis for the English that in many ways continued for the rest of the reign. Elizabeth's efforts to keep England out of foreign entanglements, which could be both dangerous and costly, failed. The difficulties and problems of continental Europe deeply influenced English policy. As the conflicts with Spain became more intense, the English perceived Spanish involvement in both the Netherlands and France as dangerous to their own security. Threatening in a different way was the possibility of foreign domination in Scotland and Ireland. Even after the defeat of the Spanish Armada in 1588, there was great concern for the rest of the reign that Philip might mount another armada. Fear of Spanish intervention in Ireland led to heightened problems there. Trying to counter Spanish influence and support for the Catholic League also meant money and English military involvement in France. The cost of these foreign policy involvements were difficult for England to bear and darkened the final decades of Elizabeth's rule. Philip II's perception of himself as "his Most Catholic Majesty" pushed religion into foreign policy for England in a way that made Elizabeth, only reluctantly a leading Protestant ruler, most uncomfortable. Spain was becoming more and more powerful, especially after 1580 when Philip had seized Portugal. In April 1581 the Portuguese Cortes formally recognized Philip as king. Catholic Spain was a serious and threatening power to Elizabeth's England.

But Spain also had its vulnerabilities to foreign powers. Francis Drake and John Hawkins had been picking off Spanish ships for a number of years. In the early 1570s Drake attacked the Spanish in the Americas and brought back some Spanish wealth to England. Though with some concerns over the repercussions, Elizabeth supported English traders who were challenging Spanish and Portuguese monopolies in West Africa, the Americas, and the East. The Queen also encouraged exploration and trade in such regions of the world as Russia and the Middle East.[2]

As relations between England and Spain soured, the privateers perceived raiding Spanish treasure ships as not only enriching, but patriotic and supportive of Protestant causes internationally. In 1580, the same year that Philip became King of Portugal, acquiring the Portuguese royal navy of 121 oceangoing galleons, Drake returned to England with his ship *The Golden Hind*. Drake had set forth in December 1577 with three ships. One was lost and the crew on another insisted on returning home. With only one ship left, Drake cruised up and down, surprising and plundering coastal towns, and eventually capturing one of the rich Spanish treasure ships that had left Peru. Drake was able to completely surprise the Spanish and then went on to the coast of California, across the Pacific, and round the Cape of Good Hope. When he arrived in Plymouth on September 26, 1580, he was the first Englishman to circumnavigate the globe. Those who had invested in his trip became wealthy; there was a return of £470 for every £1 invested and Elizabeth's share was about £160 000, half of the total takings. It is little wonder that Elizabeth went down to Plymouth herself to knight Drake on the deck of his ship in April 1581. Drake's journey enriched Elizabeth, provided information on the Pacific coast of America, and demonstrated that as powerful as Spain was, it was also assailable. Spain and the Spanish ambassador, Don Bernardino de Mendoza, were understandably outraged by Drake. Burghley and Sussex advised the Queen to disown Drake and return what he had taken to avoid war with Spain. But Leicester, Hatton, and Walsingham urged Elizabeth to ignore the Spanish protests and keep the wealth and this was exactly what Elizabeth decided to do. From then on Elizabeth, while she disclaimed any official knowledge of what they were doing, did not place any roadblocks in the way of adventurers like Drake and they were able to harass Spanish ships whenever they could, much to the fury of Spain. In the early 1580s personal relations between Mendoza and Elizabeth so deteriorated that in October 1581, Elizabeth declared she would no longer speak with him: he could only deal with Privy Councillors. But none of them were eager to spend time with Mendoza either. By the end of 1582 Mendoza complained that no one of importance would speak with him; his only contact at Court was Henry Howard. For the last year Mendoza was in England, until his expulsion in 1584 because of his intrigues, he spent his time conspiring to overthrow Elizabeth. Mendoza, instead of working to calm relations between England and Spain, was worsening the conflict. England was moving toward the Armada, what MacCaffrey has called "the definitive turning point of the Queen's reign."[3]

One of the areas where England and Spain were most at conflict was the Netherlands. William of Orange had led the resistance in the Netherlands centered in the provinces of Holland and Zeeland since 1572. The other 15 provinces had not joined in. The 1576 sack of Antwerp by Spanish soldiers resulted in a general revolt of provinces, Catholic and Calvinist alike, and the creation of a semi-independent United Netherlands. The fear of the mutinous Spanish forces, however, was what had brought together the revolutionary Calvinists of Holland and Zeeland with the conservative and Catholic nobles and magistrates of the other provinces. William of Orange tried to keep the differences from destroying them, but the various Dutch had little in common and by 1579 the rebels had split into two rival groups: the Union of Arras and the Union of Utrecht. In May 1579 the Catholic Union of Arras, which contained the provinces of Artois and Hainault, made peace with the Prince of Parma, Philip II's nephew and Governor-General in the Netherlands since the death of Don John of Austria in October 1578. Part of the peace agreement was no toleration for non-Catholics, but otherwise the ancient liberties were guaranteed, terms that were attractive to a number of provinces. Philip II was becoming more and more irritated with the trouble William of Orange was causing him. In March 1580 he issued a proclamation characterizing William as a disturber of the peace of all of Christendom but particularly the Netherlands. Philip promised a reward to any who removed this public enemy. Protestants were horrified that the King of Spain was openly inciting the murder of one of their leaders. That summer Parma ordered the governors of all the provinces to publish the proclamation. In March 1582 William was shot and for six weeks in danger of dying.

Parma was a young commander of great skill and tact and the French Duke of Anjou, trying to make his name in the Netherlands, was no match for him. The attempts at alliance with the French, which had been part of the Anjou marriage negotiation to help the Netherlands, had not been successful. William of Orange felt he had not gotten enough support from the English and turned again to the Duke of Anjou who accepted the position of governor of the States General. In 1581 under the threat of Anjou's intervention, the Arras Union asked Parma for help in defending themselves. This gave Parma a base and other provinces were soon also making peace with him, putting him in a better position to fight the Union of Utrecht. In 1582 Parma began the conquest of Flanders and Brabant, and the States General of the Utrecht Union was unable to stop him. But Anjou's Catholicism disturbed some of the Dutch Protestants, which led to bitter feelings between them. In the end Anjou was of no help; in 1583 he finally left the Netherlands to return to France where he died in June 1584.

The situation became even more desperate in the Netherlands a month later with the assassination of William of Orange. William, who had taken up residence at Delft, received a complete report of Anjou's death from a young man masquerading as Francis Guion, the son of a slain French Huguenot. He was actually Balthasar Gérard, a Catholic who was planning to kill him. Jesuit theologians had assured Gérard such a deed would be a service to the Church, and Parma had promised him that his heirs would get the reward if he was killed before he could escape after the assassination. The first time Gérard spoke to William he was unable to fulfill his commitment because he had no weapon. In his guise as loyal Protestant Gérard received from William some money to relieve his poverty; he used this money to purchase a pistol and two days later returned to the house where he shot William, this time fatally. Gérard was captured by William's guards, tortured, and then executed. At Parma's request, Philip indeed paid the reward to his parents.[4] The assassination of William left the Dutch in a critical situation. The military failure of the Utrech Union was serious enough; without William there might be no political union.

William's death had terrible ramifications not only for the Netherlands, but also for England. Also very significant and troubling was the death of the Duke of Anjou. Henry III was now the only surviving son of Henry II and the powerful Catherine de Medici. With the death of his brother, Henry III's nearest male relative, and thus the new heir to the throne, was the Protestant Henry of Navarre. The Catholic League, under the leadership of the Guise family was appalled at the thought of a Protestant successor and developed stronger ties with Spain which included a formal alliance, the Treaty of Joinville, in December 1584, accepting Philip as protector in return for funds. With the situation so uneasy in France, Henry III could do nothing to help the Dutch and soon had changed sides internationally. The Catholic League was so strong, Henry III was forced to join the alliance in July 1585 with the Treaty of Nemours.

Henry III agreed that all protection to the Huguenots would end and gave them six months to return to the Catholic faith. The King also agreed that Henry of Navarre would be excluded from the throne; instead the new heir was the elderly Cardinal of Bourbon. Henry of Navarre and his Huguenot supporters took up arms against the Catholic League. Protestants in England greatly feared that France would be completely dominated by the Catholic League and Spain, a critical situation as England and Spain were heading for war.

The Dutch, knowing no aid could come from the French, turned to the English as their last hope. By the spring of 1585 Elizabeth reluctantly realized that direct intervention by the English was necessary in the Netherlands. She agreed to take the Dutch under her protection and in August signed the Treaty of Nonesuch. As a result of the treaty, she sent the Earl of Leicester as commander and chief with 7000 English troops to aid the Dutch in their fight against Parma. Elizabeth hoped that if the Dutch were more successful, this would pressure Philip to agree to a more reasonable settlement; but for Philip, such an act of aggression meant war. He had come to believe that the root of his troubles in the Netherlands was England. The decision to support the Netherlands indeed was a commitment to fight Spain, though Elizabeth still hoped for peace and Philip did not end up sending off his Armada against England for another three years.

Once in the Netherlands Leicester made decisions that infuriated Elizabeth. She was particularly upset that he accepted the position of Governor-General, especially since this would commit England even more fully. She finally accepted the compromise that Leicester held that post under the Netherlands Estates, but not under her rule. But settling the quarrel over his title did not resolve Leicester's problems. He could not get along with either his own officers or with the Dutch, getting involved in the quarrels between the various leaders. Leicester was also continually asking Elizabeth for more money and men. Though many of the English supported the war with enthusiasm, it was not very successful and the English were distraught when Leicester's nephew Sir Philip Sidney, one of the noted courtiers and poets of his age, died in the Netherlands in October 1586. The month before, he had been wounded in the thigh in a minor skirmish at the siege of Zutphen and the wound had caused gangrene. Sidney's death was a particular waste. He had been wounded because of his refusal to wear armor into battle: his commander had a minor wound and could not wear his armor, and Sidney had stated he would be disgraced to go into battle wearing more armor than his commander. Thousands of mourners attended Sidney's funeral at St Paul's the following February.

At the end of 1586 Leicester was summoned back to England to explain the situation in the Netherlands. He left Sir John Norris, his most able commander, in charge of the English forces. With Leicester's approval, Elizabeth had sent Sir William Stanley to hold the town of Deventer. Though Stanley was Catholic, he had served her loyally in Ireland and she and Leicester ignored the protests of the Dutch Protestants to have a Catholic in such a position. Unfortunately, the Dutch were right. In January 1587 Stanley surrendered Deventer to Parma; the same day, another English soldier, Rowland Yorke, surrendered an important fortress near Zutphen. Stanley, who turned out to have been in secret correspondence with Elizabeth's Catholic enemies for some years, received £50 000 from Parma for his treachery. The Dutch were outraged that they had incurred such losses because of the treason committed by Englishmen. They blamed Elizabeth for not listening to their warnings against trusting Catholics.

The Privy Council wanted Leicester to return to the Netherlands with more men and greater financial backing, though as late as 1587 Elizabeth still hoped to avoid war with Spain and was concerned about England's role in the Netherlands. The Dutch were also more and more distrustful of their English allies. But when Parma besieged Sluys in June, Elizabeth recognized that something needed to be done and agreed to send Leicester back to the Netherlands with 5000 men and £30 000. Unfortunately, though it was not his fault, Sluys fell to the Spanish and Leicester still found it impossible to get along with the Dutch leaders. Elizabeth and Walsingham became convinced that Leicester's presence was not of much help, but though Elizabeth still pursued the idea of peace and was attempting to negotiate, Walsingham was convinced that to abandon the Dutch would have disastrous consequences for England. Leicester finally returned to England in December 1587 and resigned all his authority in the Netherlands. His successor, Peregrine Bertie, Lord Willoughby, had a much more limited role. Even with the fighting going on, in February 1585 Elizabeth had appointed a commission to negotiate with Parma's agents and they continued to discuss peace terms for the Netherlands until their departure in July 1588, after Philip had already dispatched his Armada. What kept Elizabeth's representatives and Parma from ever agreeing was Elizabeth's demand that Philip grant religious toleration to the Dutch. In July 1588 the English envoys finally returned home. Though war was now imminent between England and Spain, the situation had actually improved in the Netherlands. Parma was so busy mobilizing troops for the invasion of England, he had no time to mount a serious campaign against the Dutch and without Leicester there to stir up dissent, the Dutch leadership was able to work together more effectively.

As relations with Spain deteriorated, England was concerned with the Netherlands and France. But Ireland also continued to cause anxiety, as did Scotland. The problems in Ireland only worsened.[5] The Irish community in the Pale were relieved in 1579 that Sir Henry Sidney had been recalled, but then, the same year, there was a major insurrection in Munster led originally by James Fitzmaurice, and after his death in August 1579 by John Fitzgerald, Earl of Desmond. The rebellion spread into the Pale itself when Viscount Baltinglass rose in revolt in the southwestern Pale. The English feared the leaders were getting support from Philip of Spain and Pope Gregory XIII, who sent to Ireland Dr Nicholas Sanders, the eminent English Catholic priest in exile, as his emissary. The Pope also dispatched soldiers, mostly of Italian birth though some Spaniards, led by Fitzmaurice, who had been in Spain. Fitzmaurice and his men landed at Smerwick July 1579 and constructed a fort there, while Sanders was sending out letters rallying the Irish to the papal banner against Elizabeth. Eventually 600 Italian and Spanish troops joined the fort at Smerwick. Sir Nicholas Malby, who had been fighting in Ireland since the mid-1560s and had been appointed president of Connaught, wrote to Lord Burghley in July 1580 that the landing of only "twenty Spaniards will drive all the Irish into rebellion."[6] Arthur, Lord Grey de Wilton led a force of 8000 men to restore order, taking the fort at Smerwick, which surrendered in expectation of mercy in November. Grey, however, ordered the massacre of the entire garrison. As the rebellion gained support, there was great brutality and accusations of atrocities on both sides. Sir William Pelham seized Desmond's estates and killed anyone he could find there. He ordered his men to dig up the tombs of Desmond's ancestors and scatter their remains. The rebellion spread to the previous loyal families in the Pale, upsetting England even more.

Grey's policy was one of scorched earth in Munster, deliberately destroying the arable land and executing many members of prominent Pale families often, suggests Palmer, on the flimsiest of evidence. Members of Elizabeth's government were extremely concerned that the rebellion was continuing; Grey's policy, however, was brutal but effective. But Elizabeth was disturbed over how virulent and vicious he was being. In 1582 she recalled Grey and, despite his objections, granted a general pardon to the rebels while placing a price on Desmond's head. This proved an effective policy; Desmond was eventually captured and killed in November 1583 and the rebellion was over. But the rebellion had been significant and disturbing. Though the foreign intervention had been minimal, that the intervention had materialized at all made such future possibilities even more frightening. Spain, upset with Drake's appropriations of treasure ships, found Elizabeth unwilling to discuss the matter with the ambassador Mendoza because of Spanish support of Ireland. Also, the financial cost to England had been staggering just at a time when the demands on England to aid the Netherlands were also at their height.[7] In the mid-1580s Elizabeth and her Council had little time or finances for Ireland and instructed the Lord Deputies to economize and keep Ireland quiet. For a while this strategy actually worked quite well.[8]

At the beginning of the 1570s Scotland, as well as Ireland, had caused considerable concern for the English. In January 1570 the Regent Moray was assassinated and the following year his replacement Lennox was also murdered. Elizabeth supported the new Regent, the Earl of Mar. By the early 1570s Elizabeth had lost all sympathy with Mary and, instead of working to protect her, now wished to return her to Scotland not as limited Queen, but to be put on trial for Darnley's murder and executed. But since she was unwilling to have this known publicly and the Scottish lords, on the other hand, would only consider such a proposal with Elizabeth's complicity in the plan made public, Mary stayed in England. Elizabeth now thoroughly supported the Protestants in Scotland; even though she was again reluctant over the expense, in 1573 she sent William Drury with an English force to help Mar's successor James Douglas, Earl of Morton, take Edinburgh castle, the last garrison held by Mary's supporters. For the next five years, Scotland was relatively quiet and there were positive relations between Scotland and England. This changed, however, in the late 1570s and for some time there was a struggle for power in Scotland, and serious concern in England over what that would mean.

The Guise family in France still had hopes for winning over Scotland and then using it as a base for conquering England. They had close ties with Scottish Catholic refugees in Paris and encouraged Jesuits to go to Scotland as well as England at great risk to find converts to Catholicism. The Guises were also secretly in touch with a number of the Scottish lords, not only Catholic, but Protestants who would be happy to destroy Morton. In March 1578 the Earl of Atholl attempted to overthrow Morton, calling a council of lords who removed him from the position of Regent and declared that James VI at the age of 12 was ready to rule.

Elizabeth was furious about this turn of events, but before she decided what would be the best course of action, Morton was uneasily back in control with the aid of the young Earl of Mar. Morton no longer called himself Regent, but he still was able to wield some power. The next year the Scottish Catholics in exile in France working with the Duke of Guise decided on another stratagem, encouraging James's French cousin, Esmé Stuart, Sieur of Aubigny, to visit Scotland and try to influence his young relative. He was soon intimate with James and able to exert great sway over his royal cousin. Aubigny's conversion to the reformed religion at that time was probably, as Jasper Ridley suggests, a political trick the Guises had suggested.[9] James appointed his cousin Earl (eventually Duke) of Lennox.

All that year Morton's influence was waning as Lennox became more and more powerful. By the spring of 1580 Burghley and Walsingham were alarmed about the political/religious situation in the North, afraid that Scotland would be dominated by Catholics in alliance with France or Spain. Lennox did soon make a move against what Burghley and Walsingham perceived to be English interests. At the end of December 1580, Lennox stood up in Council and accused Morton of having been involved in the murder of James's father, Lord Darnley, 14 years earlier. For over a decade the accusation of involvement in Darnley's murder had been the way those in power had destroyed those they opposed. Morton himself had used it against his enemies. Since virtually all the Scottish lords had been happy to see Darnley dead, it was an easy accusation to make. Morton was imprisoned in Edinburgh Castle until his trial. This move against Morton alarmed Elizabeth and her Council, who perceived it as the beginning of Catholic plans to take over Scotland and then England. As soon as Elizabeth learned of the arrest, she sent Thomas Randolph to Scotland with orders that he demand not only the release of Morton but the exile of Lennox. Elizabeth also ordered Henry Carey, Baron Hunsdon, to be ready to cross the border with an army of 2500 if necessary.

Randolph found it impossible to successfully negotiate with the Scottish Privy Council. They rejected his demands and moved Morton so it would be more difficult for Randolph to attempt to aid him in escaping. Randolph was afraid that if the English did invade, they would meet a unified Scotland and Morton would be immediately killed. Instead, he negotiated secretly with Morton's kinsman Archibald Douglas, the Earl of Angus. The plan was to assassinate Lennox and the Earls of Argyll and of Montrose, who were also sympathetic to Mary Stuart. After getting rid of their enemies, Angus would take control of young James, release Morton, and restore him to power.

Elizabeth reluctantly agreed that the plotters might "surprise" Lennox, as long as they did not do so in the King's presence. If she understood that "surprise" meant to murder, she did not give any indication of it. Nor was she aware that Lennox was not the only target. But before the plot could be carried out, one of the conspirators betrayed the plan to the Scottish government. Randolph and Angus managed to escape, and Randolph was convinced that now the only way to save Morton and further English interests was invasion. Elizabeth, however, decided against invasion, fearing that the French would see it as a hostile move. Nothing could save Morton, who was tried and executed in June. Morton denied participation in Darnley's death though he admitted that he had been aware that Bothwell had intended the murder.

In August 1582 the Earls of Gowrie and Mar, in a plot Walsingham was certainly aware of and may have organized, kidnapped James VI and took him to Ruthven Castle. Lennox's influence in Scotland was over and he returned to France. A year later James, now 17, escaped and with the help of the Earl of Arran took control. Two months later he had Gowrie executed for treason for organizing the Raid of Ruthven. Elizabeth gave up trying to support a pro-English party in Scotland, but relations did not deteriorate in the way Walsingham feared. James wanted to inherit the English throne and did not want to alienate its present occupant. The situation became more fraught in 1586 as there was yet one more Catholic conspiracy to place James's mother Mary Stuart on the throne of England. Though James had not seen his mother since he was an infant, and she could stand in the way of his own place in the English succession, for him to acquiesce in her execution placed him in a difficult situation. James was under great public pressure to save Mary, and then after her death in February 1587 to avenge her. But James, in the end, was glad to accept Elizabeth's assurances that her Secretary William Davison had sent on the death warrant without her permission and that his mother's treason did not impugn his claim to the English throne. Mary's execution inflamed the Guises in France. Though James was her son, she bequeathed her claim to the English throne to Philip and her death moved his invasion one step closer. But the Netherlands, France, and Ireland were still trouble spots as England moved toward war with Spain. At least relationships with Scotland had calmed down despite the death of Mary Stuart.

In late 1587 Elizabeth tried to convince Henry III, who chafed under his domination by the Catholic League, to openly break with them and throw his support to Henry of Navarre and the Huguenots, who had won a notable battle at Coutras in October. Her ambassador to France, Sir Edward Stafford, did his best to persuade the French King that this would be in his own best interests. By early the next year, Henry met secretly with Stafford and he begged the English Queen to induce Navarre to convert to Catholicism, which would rob the Guises of their main argument against him. While Elizabeth could not promise this, she did offer Henry help against the League if he would arrest the leading Guises as traitors and break openly with the League; this plan, however, made Henry III much too nervous, though he was distressed with the power wielded by the Duke of Guise. In the meantime, the Spanish were encouraging the Guises to engineer a Catholic rebellion in France. In early May the Duke of Guise entered Paris and seized control. A revolutionary Committee of Sixteen, who ardently supported the Guises and the Catholic League, ruled the city while the King ignominiously fled to Chartres. But instead of joining with Elizabeth and Navarre and attempting with Huguenot support to retake Paris from the rebels, within a few weeks Henry III had decided to negotiate with the League. By July the King had completely capitulated to them once again, swearing to exterminate the Huguenots, to have no heretic succeed him, and to denounce any alliance with the English. Elizabeth's efforts to turn Henry III away from the League failed, but at least the Huguenot party was still strong enough to keep France from joining Spain against England.

While Elizabeth's government had to deal with problems in France, the Netherlands, Ireland and Scotland, Sir Francis Drake was determined that the Spanish would not have a navy to send against England. In April 1587 by order of the Queen, Drake set out with a fleet of ships. The Spanish commander Santa Cruz had the main body of galleons in Lisbon, but there were more ships at Cadiz and this is where Drake headed, his task to disrupt and delay Spanish preparations. Drake, appalled by how much Philip had already accomplished to prepare for the invasion, swept into the Cadiz harbor and destroyed between two and three dozen of the larger ships there, and sent back word to England that it needed to prepare strongly against Philip. Elizabeth, still hoping for peace, had sent a messenger to Drake with new orders telling him not to attack, but Drake had got to sea before these new orders had caught up with him and he made his raid. When the English heard, they were delighted; Drake's raid delayed the Armada by a year. He also captured a Spanish ship, the *San Felipe*, one of Philip's own, carrying a cargo worth £140 000. This not only provided a financial gain for the

English, but also forced Santa Cruz to move his fleet from cruising near Lisbon to the Azores to protect the bullion. The English had gained additional time to prepare for their defense. Philip had intended the Armada to set sail in the summer of 1587, but he finally reluctantly admitted that because of Drake's destruction of the fleet it had to be delayed.[10] In early 1588 Philip had his Armada refitted, and appointed the Duke of Medina Sidonia to replace Santa Cruz when he died in February.

Drake had delayed the Armada, but in 1588 it was clear this was the year Spain would attempt the "enterprise of England," to conquer the country and return it to the Catholic faith.[11] The Spanish fleet consisted of 65 first line galleons, and an equal number of lesser vessels. These could carry 18 000 troops and 7000 sailors. In Flanders, Parma had 55 000 foot soldiers and 5000 cavalry: 17 000 troops were sent to assemble in the ports of Flanders, so that the Spanish would have 35 000 troops for the invasion of England.

Preparing for the Spanish Armada was expensive and difficult. Lord Admiral Charles Howard of Effingham and John Hawkins, as Treasurer of the Navy, had been hard at work and by 1588 Elizabeth had 34 ships, 19 of which were major fighting vessels. There were also about 40 privateering vessels which would come to the Queen's aid. The royal ships were commanded and manned with freelance captains and crew who were temporarily in the Queen's pay. The land forces were less well organized, though there had been mobilization and deployment of forces focused upon several important ports and plans for defending forces and guarding the Queen. Elizabeth and her Council had a balancing act in terms of how long they could keep men mobilized and did not do so during the winter months of 1587 and early 1588. Convinced that Drake had indeed delayed the Armada and that Philip would not be sending it in the winter, Elizabeth saved her money for the spring. It was a highly anxious time.

As the time for the Armada approached, English Catholic refugees abroad were jubilant, convinced that Elizabeth would be overthrown and England brought back to the Catholic Church. Some looked for help from their co-religionists at home. But, in fact, England united behind its Queen in a great show of nationalism. In the summer of 1588 Elizabeth was at her most popular and many Catholics were prepared to place patriotism above religion and fight loyally for their Queen and country. The English realized that the Armada planned to sail up the Channel and meet up with Parma's forces for the invasion of England. In preparation, 22 000 men were assembled in a camp near Tilbury to stop Parma before he could reach London. All the other land forces were to stay in their counties in a state of readiness and preparations were made to light beacons on hilltops to give warning. Lord Howard was Lord Admiral, in supreme command of the navy with Drake as his second in command. Elizabeth was at Richmond, serene in her view that God would support the English.

After all the preparation and waiting, the Armada set sail from Lisbon in late May, though a storm soon scattered the ships and forced Medina Sidonia to wait for a month at Corunna, just beyond Cape Finisterre, until his ships were reunited. He then had to refit and supply the ships. Medina Sidonia wrote to Philip suggesting that, even at this late date, the enterprise be abandoned, but Philip refused to consider it. By the third week of July the Armada left Corunna and seven days later was sighted by the English. At Plymouth Lord Howard and Drake prepared to attack the Armada and were able to destroy some of the ships. Elizabeth, to be closer to London, moved to her palace at St James. The English also engaged the Spanish on 2 and 4 August, off the Isle of Wight. Medina Sidonia took the rest of his fleet to Calais while he waited for news of Parma and his forces, arriving there on 6 August. One of the problems experienced in the Armada was the miscommunications between Medina Sidonia and Parma. Meanwhile, Drake and Howard assembled 150 ships to fight the Spanish. Drake decided to use eight fireships against them: he set the ships on fire and sent them into the Armada, which caused great panic among the Spanish. As they saw the burning ships approaching, a number of Spanish ships hurriedly cut their cables and went out to sea. None of the fireships succeeded in exploding before they drifted to shore; nor did they set fire to any of the Armada vessels. But they accomplished what Drake wanted. Medina Sidonia, seeing some of his ships leave, ordered the rest of the fleet to follow. Off Gravelines, Drake then attacked them and they were thoroughly scattered or destroyed. Nearly half the Spanish ships were too damaged to continue fighting and the others were too demoralized.[12]

The English soon realized they had had a victory but did not yet understand its magnitude. When Leicester invited her to visit her army at Tilbury, she believed that the Armada might be able to regroup and still invade. Despite the concern of some of her Councillors that this placed her in too much danger, Elizabeth decided to accept the invitation. Her speech to the troops is one of the most famous that she delivered. She assured them:

I have always so behaved myself that, under God, I have placed my chiefest strength and safeguard in the loyal hearts and good will of my subjects, and therefore I am come amongst you as you see, at this time, not for my recreation and disport, but being resolved, in the midst and heart of the battle, to live or die amongst you all, to lay down for my God, and for my kingdom, and for my people, my honour and my blood, even in the dust. I know I have the body of a weak and feeble woman, but I have the heart and stomach of a King, and of a King of England too, and think foul scorn that Parma or Spain or any Prince of Europe should dare to invade the borders of my realm.[13]

While Elizabeth was still at Tilbury news arrived that the Armada had been defeated and the danger of invasion was over, at least for the time being. While England was safe, Elizabeth and her Council were all too slow in paying her sailors and soldiers. At first, rumors spread of Philip's victory to the delight of the Spanish Ambassador Mendoza, now living in Paris, and the Pope, who had ordered a victory *Te Deum* be sung in St Peter's. But eventually Philip learned just how devastating the defeat of his Armada had been. Rather than giving up, he decided to intensify the war against the heretics. He promised to build a new and stronger fleet to renew his "enterprise" the following year. Fear of further Armadas darkened the 1590s.

In hindsight we know that the Armada never landed and that the chance for success for the Spanish was not strong. But though Medina Sidonia might have recognized the chancy nature of the enterprise, claiming that the Spanish were sailing in "confident hope of a miracle," for the English it was a time of great trial. Geoffrey Parker and Colin Martin suggest that "England's best-informed opinion in 1588 was . . . not disposed to underestimate the enormity of the threat which Philip II's great Armada had posed." Penry Williams argues that while the Armada's chance of success was not high, neither was it negligible. He goes on to point out that the consequences of the Armada are difficult to sort out, though had the Armada succeeded England's history would have been far different. The Netherlands would also have been at far greater risk.[14]

But it is also clear that the English defeat of the Spanish Armada in 1588 did not resolve everything. Wernham suggests that "for the English it was indeed a famous victory . . . The moral effect, the boost to national confidence was great,"[15] and certainly the 1590s were a time of impressive cultural achievement. That decade was also, however, a time when problems with Ireland grew more demanding and there was ever greater concern that Spain would come to Ireland's aid against England, which indeed did happen with the Tyrone rebellion. England was also still involved in the Netherlands and France, and the costs of defense and foreign involvement were heavy. There was serious concern about another Armada, and indeed Philip sent further fleets against England in 1596 and 1597; luckily for the English, they were driven back by storms. Paralleling the delight people felt in the achievements of Shakespeare, Marlowe, and Spenser were the poor harvests, the inflation, and the general anxiety of the end of the sixteenth century.

For the rest of Elizabeth's reign, she was often reluctant about continuing England's expensive foreign policy commitments, but Burghley believed that unless the Netherlands were kept secure and the French King supported against the Catholic League, it would be a disaster for England. Some of her younger advisors, especially Leicester's step-son, the Earl of Essex, wanted to see further attacks on Spain, especially if this were to yield more treasure. There were often clashes of opinion. The conflicting views meant that English policy and strategy were often complex and changeable. The scarcity of resources also created difficulties and the government's financial troubles continued to grow more intense. In the 1590s occasional profits that came from privateers did not off-set the costs of war.

Despite some common interests, as we have seen, relations between the English and Dutch had been problematic in the mid-1580s and continued to deteriorate after the defeat of the Armada. The Dutch were upset over just how much aid and how many men the English were willing to dispatch, and also angered by what they saw as English interference in the domestic politics of the Low Countries. In the spring of 1589, Parma's successes seriously threatened Dutch resistance. Fortunately for the Dutch, Parma became ill and his men unhappy, which slowed operations. The appointment of Sir Francis Vere to replace Peregrine Bertie, Lord Willoughby, in August 1589, to lead the English army in the Netherlands also improved relations. Vere was not only a capable soldier, but also showed tact and good sense and got along well with Maurice of Nassau, in command of the Dutch armies. By 1590 Parma's forces were being diverted to France because of the crisis there and the threat to the Netherlands receded. English attention and concern shifted away from the Netherlands to France.

If relations with the Dutch were problematic, so were those with the Kings of France. Before the Armada Elizabeth had tried to stiffen Henry III's resolve against the Guises but with little success. From the summer of 1588 Henry had in fact been strongly under the influence of Henry, Duke of Guise, who had become his chief minister and ally. But Henry, though Guise was not aware of it, was tired of Guise's domination and decided, with the aid of trusted bodyguards, to deal with the issue once and for all. On December 23, 1588, he had Guise murdered at Blois, where the Court was in residence. The next day Guise's brother, the Cardinal of Lorraine, also in attendance at Blois, was arrested and strangled. Henry hoped to also assassinate the third brother, the Duke of Mayenne, who was at Lyons. He was warned, however, that murderers had been dispatched and fled to Paris, where he and his sister, the Duchess of Montpensier, rallied the faithful to avenge the death of the Catholic martyr, the Duke of Guise. Henry III's mother, Catherine de Medici, who died only two weeks after the assassination of Guise, worried that what Henry had done would cost him his throne.

Paris was soon in an uproar. The divinity faculty of the University of Paris declared that by such action Henry III had forfeited his crown and there were demands that the Pope excommunicate him. Some claimed that the death of Guise was an even worse blow to Philip II than the loss of his soldiers in the Armada. Parma began to prepare to bring his forces to France to support the Catholic League. Huguenots in France, however, were jubilant about the news of Guise's death, and Elizabeth wrote Henry a letter of congratulation and again urged him to ally himself with his loyal subjects, the Huguenots.

Henry had hated Guise, but he did not murder him to secure the support of the Protestants. Rather, he had hoped that Catholics who had disliked the Duke of Guise and the League would rally to his support. He publicly labeled Guise a traitor who had deserved execution since he had been trying to deprive Henry of his crown. But Henry also assured the French people of his hatred of heretics. In fact, he said, had he not been distracted by Guise he would have done more against them. He called on all his loyal subjects to unite with him against the Huguenots. But Henry could not defeat the League without the aid of the Huguenots and he began to negotiate with Henry of Navarre. In April they officially reconciled and announced their joint venture against the rebels in the League. Henry III asked Elizabeth for £80 000 so that he might hire mercenaries as the League had done. Her Councillors were unanimous in arguing that the English should support Henry; Elizabeth finally agreed to give him £20 000 and underwrite a loan for the rest. But Henry would not be there to receive the loan. On August 1 a monk named Jacques Clément stated he could show the King a secret way into

Paris for his army. When brought into Henry III's presence, he attempted to stab the king instead. In the struggle Henry managed to kill the monk, but died hours later from his own wounds. But though Henry of Navarre proclaimed himself Henry IV and promised to uphold the Catholic faith in France, many Catholics refused to support a Huguenot king and the League countered by presenting an alternative: Cardinal Bourbon was proclaimed Charles X.

Elizabeth recognized that it was crucial to continue to aid France. She agreed to loan Henry an additional £20 000. She also dispatched Lord Willoughby, recently returned from the Netherlands, to support Henry's campaign in Normandy with 4000 men. The support proved successful and Willoughby returned home. By March of 1590 Henry had destroyed the League's field army and had moved to Paris. Only Parma's timely arrival saved the city from Henry. But while Henry might have been able to fight the League, he could not successfully battle the League and Philip. While Henry could have fought the League successfully on his own, he could not do that once Philip had decided to give the League substantial aid. The English saw Parma's army in France and the arrival of Spanish troops in Brittany in October 1590 as a direct threat. If they successfully defeated Henry, this would be a base for the renewed attempt to invade England.

In 1591 and 1592 England was involved in both the Netherlands and France. Elizabeth provided some funding and men in the Netherlands, where the Protestants were proving successful in their fight against Spain. Sir Francis Vere worked well with Maurice of Nassau and Parma was constantly distracted by Philip's orders that he march into France. Elizabeth was also providing money and men to Henry IV of France at the same time, but with less success. The Earl of Essex in his first independent command attempted to aid Henry IV in the siege of Rouen. Parma was supporting Rouen against Henry's forces. But despite the long campaign, the Catholics held on to Rouen and it was becoming clear to Henry that he could not continue to fight the Spanish unless he had much more support than Elizabeth was willing to give. And the French campaigns were highly unpopular at home with many of the English forces deserting their posts.[16] The only way Henry could woo the moderate Catholics at home away from the League and gain their loyalty was to convert. In May he announced he was willing to receive instruction and two months later was received into the Roman Catholic Church. Henry had obviously seen what was necessary; by the next year he had taken Paris and was soon to have the allegiance of all but a small minority of nobles still loyal to the

League. Perhaps Elizabeth was not surprised by Henry's conversion. She was certainly not pleased, but it is difficult to see what else Henry could have done and even though he was now a Catholic, it was still in England's interest to support him against the Spanish. Although Henry had settled the internal dissentions in France, he still had to deal with the armies of Spain; in 1595 Henry declared open war. England was also still at war with Spain, and Lord Howard of Effington and the Earl of Essex convinced Elizabeth to make a pre-emptive strike on the Spanish fleet at Cadiz. But while this was still in the planning stage the situation in France became more critical.

Though Henry had effectively defeated the Catholic League, the Spanish had taken Cambrai in late 1595. Henry urgently asked for more aid, but Elizabeth refused and to the great dismay of England, Henry, as a means of applying pressure, suggested that he might make a separate peace with Spain. By spring of 1596 the Spanish army had reached Calais and were besieging the city. The threat to England felt serious if Calais should fall and some in England thought the Cadiz expedition should be sent to Calais instead. But Elizabeth wanted Calais back in English hands if the English were to aid in its rescue. While she was negotiating this with the French, Calais fell to the Spanish. Soon after, Elizabeth agreed to an alliance with Henry. She was concerned about France, but also about how much she could help; the situation in Ireland was also swallowing men and resources. Meanwhile, while the Cadiz expedition had been a success, it had also missed opportunities and did not return with the wealth Elizabeth had hoped. It did, however, infuriate Philip enough that he planned to send another Armada the next year, which caused the English great worry. Ninety-eight ships were dispatched, but they were hit by heavy storms that sank a third of them. The rest struggled back to port and Philip had to abandon the enterprise again. Briefly, France, England, and the Netherlands joined together against Spain, but each of their interests was too different. In September 1597 Henry IV recaptured Amiens and was in a strong position to negotiate with the Spanish. The Dutch did not want a treaty since the Spanish were unwilling to agree to their freedoms, and Elizabeth and Burghley believed that Henry was rushing too fast given the complexities of the issues. Burghley's son Robert Cecil was dispatched with Dutch envoys to express concern over what Spanish domination of the Netherlands might mean, but Henry felt no allegiance to his allies and did not want to hurt his own position out of regard for the English. Cecil wrote Elizabeth that "France will be France, and leave his best friends."[17] Soon after Cecil left France, Henry made peace with Spain.

Elizabeth had other worries besides the fickleness of the French King. The situation in Ireland was worsening.[18] At the beginning of the last decade of the sixteenth century, Ireland appeared to be fairly stable under English authority. Outside of Ulster, English local administration had garrisons and a system of government that could contain and localize disturbances. Tudor rule may have seemed effectively to be a military occupation, argues Steven Ellis, but the "English armies had apparently adjusted to the difficult terrain of Gaelic Ireland," and the English were firmly in control.[19] But the English settlers hated the Irish with the same intensity as the Irish hated them. Many of the English were convinced, they said, that God intended Ireland for them.

In the 1590s, reducing the authority of the Gaelic lords in Ulster was the natural next move. English officials in Ireland hoped that breaking up the traditional Gaelic overlordships, such as Tyrone's, would release yet more land for English plantations. In Ulster power was divided between Turlough Luineach O'Neill, chief of the clan, Hugh O'Neill, Baron Dungannon, created Earl of Tyrone in 1585, and his son-in-law Hugh Roe O'Donnell in Tirconnell. For a long time the O'Donnells had been enemies of the O'Neills, but they had come to an alliance when Hugh Roe married Rose O'Neill. In May 1593 Turlough resigned in Tyrone's favor, though he did formally lead the clan until Turlough's death two years later. Tyrone, one of the most powerful of the Gaelic lords, had reached an accommodation with the crown in 1579 that lasted almost a decade. When Spanish sailors and soldiers were shipwrecked in Ireland after the Armada, Tyrone took an active part in obeying English orders and killing all he could find. But under the English Lord Deputy Sir William Fitzwillian, who replaced John Perrot in 1588, the Dublin government was taking power away from the Gaelic lords in Ulster. This was done in part to have it under tighter control, but another motive was to satisfy the ambitions of English settlers such as Sir Nicholas Bagenal, marshall of the army, and his son Henry. Hostility between the Gaelic lords and the English was made worse by the personal rivalry of Tyrone and Henry Bagenal. In the 1590s Tyrone would lead the most serious revolt of the sixteenth century against English rule, what historians have called the Nine Years' War. This disastrous military struggle allowed England to complete the conquest, to finally accomplish the establishment of English sovereignty throughout Ireland.

Hiram Morgan calls Hugh O'Neill, the Earl of Tyrone, "one of the most adept politicians in Irish history."[20] Hugh O'Neill was born about 1550. After his father Matthew, Lord Dungannon, was killed by orders of Shane O'Neill in 1558, Hugh became a ward of the English crown and his wardship granted to Giles Hovenden, an Englishman living in the Pale. Though Hovenden was a Protestant, this apparently did not make a large impression on O'Neill. In 1584 O'Neill signaled his adherence to Catholicism by celebrating Easter according to Pope Gregory's new-style calendar. Conformity to Protestantism would not have been a politically adept move for Gaelic lords such as O'Neill because an important adjunct to their power was the influence they exercised over the local church. Certainly by 1594 O'Neill was publicly known as a papist. In 1562 Hugh's older brother Brian was killed, leaving Hugh and Cormac as the surviving legitimate sons of Lord Dungannon. It was only in 1566, when war broke out between the crown and Shane O'Neill, that Hugh acquired some importance in the political arena. At this point Lord Deputy Henry Sidney began to pay attention to Hugh and may have entertained him in the viceregal household. But Morgan argues that there is no evidence whatsoever that Hugh was brought to the Sidney home at Penhurst, and that the statement that Hugh was educated in England is a false legend.[21] Rather than being trained in the refined graces of a courtier, argues Morgan, O'Neill received a basic education and had the same exposure to English attitudes as any other young Gaelic noble. Still, his upbringing was of great advantage to him as it gave him a sense of familiarity in both Irish and English cultures. When he visited the English Court in 1587, he made a favorable impression on Elizabeth and was on good terms with Leicester and Walsingham.

At the end of the decade of the 1580s, there were two connected administrative developments that signified the advance of the crown government in northern Ireland: the English created a northern assize circuit that eventually brought royal justice into the localities on a regular basis. This threatened the authority of the Gaelic lords in general, but a later development was a particular threat to O'Neill. The rulings made at the assizes had to be enforced and in June 1591 a commission was established in Ulster to take care of this. The assize judges were named as some of the assistant commissioners and the Privy Council named Sir Henry Bagenal chief commissioner; a year earlier the Queen had appointed him to both his father's office of marshall of the army and seat on the Irish council. Fitzwilliam was clearly behind Bagenal's rise in power. In an attempt to balance this power, in 1591 Hugh O'Neill asked

Sir Henry if he might make Henry's sister Mabel his third wife. When Bagenal refused, the two eloped,[22] and Hugh clearly hoped that his new brother-in-law would accept the *fait accompli*. Sir Henry did not; the money her father had set aside for Mabel's dowry was not paid for some years and the relations between the two men were more hostile than ever. In 1593 Fitzwilliam commissioned Tyrone to work with Marshal Bagenal against the rebel Maguire. But Bagenal refused to recognize Tyrone's assistance and the Earl felt ill-used, convinced that Bagenal and Fitzwilliam were conspiring against him. In 1594 Fitzwilliam was replaced by Sir William Russell.

Tyrone secretly worked to draw together a confederacy of Gaelic lords who would attempt to regain authority in their territories. Because of an old family feud, he, in violation of the law and the Queen's authority, seized Shane O'Neill's son and hanged him. The Council in Dublin advised Elizabeth to come to some agreement with Tyrone, but the Queen would not agree. By early 1595 he was in open rebellion and gaining a force of trained volunteers. He defeated his old enemy and brother-in-law Sir Henry Bagenal at Clontibret. The English government ordered troops in Brittany to head to Ireland. Tyrone and his men were able to withdraw into the forests. Ulster appeared to be unconquerable. Tyrone began to negotiate with the Pope and Philip II for support, and posed a greater threat to the English control of Ireland than any Irish lord previously that century.

Elizabeth decided to negotiate with Tyrone and offered him a pardon and substantial local control under certain conditions. Tyrone agreed to negotiate, at least to provide himself with a breathing space. He agreed to accept Elizabeth's pardon and pay a fine, but Tyrone and his son-in-law O'Donnell were also demanding liberty of conscience for Catholics in Ireland, which the Protestants were not willing to grant. Tyrone was convinced that he could not trust Elizabeth, or any of the English, and was biding his time until he started a new insurrection and continued his correspondence with Philip who was encouraging the rebellion.

In July 1598 Tyrone attacked and besieged the garrison at the Black-water Fort near Dungannon. Tyrone and his men then attacked the force from Armagh led by Sir Henry Bagenal that came to relieve the garrison and defeated them near the Yellow Ford. Nearly half of the royal army including Bagenal was killed and some of the Irish serving in the English army deserted to join the rebels. The Irish rebels were delighted by their victory, which had shocked the English. Elizabeth decided to send 2000 soldiers then serving in the Netherlands to Ireland and urged the Lord

Deputy in Ireland to enlist no more Irish to serve in the army. All too often, Irish soldiers could desert to the rebels and Tyrone's success had spread far beyond Ulster. The English government in Ireland was convinced that the rebels had supporters in every town, who were providing them with supplies. O'Donnell had gained most of Connacht and the Munster rebels drove most of the English settlers out. One English officer wished for portable racks so wherever they were, the local army officers could torture the locals to obtain information about the rebels.[23] By the fall of 1598 the English had lost control of all of Ireland except for Leinster. Ireland had become a top priority and preoccupation of the English government. The question was what to do about it.

Most of the men Elizabeth most counted on for advice throughout her reign were gone. Leicester died in 1588, soon after the defeat of the Armada. Walsingham died in 1590. Lord Burghley was the only one left and his health was failing; his death in 1598 had heightened tensions at Elizabeth's court as his son Robert Cecil and Robert Devereux, Earl of Essex, struggled for control. Essex did not want anyone to gain glory and credit in Ireland, and ended up so limiting the choices that he had to go himself. But the risks for him – and for England – were great. Elizabeth gave Essex an army of over 16 000 men, the largest that had ever been sent to Ireland, and he left London in March 1599. Unfortunately, Essex was able to accomplish nothing in Ireland. He was, for all his great boasts, not a brilliant soldier, did not understand Irish warfare, and did not have a clear strategy. Despite his large force, he did not have what he needed to defeat Tyrone; he wasted time and exhausted his men trying unsuccessfully to subdue Munster and Limerick. In August, at Elizabeth's command, he marched against Tyrone, leading a force of 4000 men, though advisors in Ireland itself thought it a poor idea. Tyrone, at the northern border of the Pale had a much larger force and Essex was convinced that the English would lose terribly were a battle fought. Instead, Essex met privately with Tyrone, leading people to wonder what they had actually said to each other. A truce followed, with the rebels holding on to their conquests and a pardon promised for Tyrone if he submitted to Elizabeth's authority. This was not what Elizabeth had in mind when she sent Essex to Ireland.

Elizabeth had commanded Essex not to leave his post, but in late September he left Dublin for her Court, where he rushed in to give her his explanation for what had – and had not – transpired in Ireland. Essex's failure in Ireland would have great repercussions for both him and the end of Elizabeth's reign. And Ireland was more problematic than ever.

Tyrone would not submit unless religious freedom was guaranteed, which the English refused to grant. In February 1600 Charles Blount, Lord Mountjoy, arrived in Ireland accompanied by Sir George Carew, the new Lord President of Munster. Unlike Essex, Mountjoy was able to eventually defeat Tyrone and the rebellion; he acted with determination and, with the support of his commanders, using both guile and force, began a successful war of intimidation and starvation. They crushed the rebellion in the southwest and Tyrone realized he could only succeed if he had real support from the Spanish. Philip III, now King of Spain since the death of his father in 1598, agreed to send some men. Tyrone sent word that if the force were large enough, 6000 men or more, it should land at Waterford or Cork, but a smaller force should go north. The Spanish commander, Don Juan del Aguila, given the smaller size of his army, wanted to land at Donegal Bay, where the rebels could easily join him. But the Catholic Archbishop of Dublin, the link between Spain and the rebels, overruled him and in October 1601 the Spanish force landed at Kinsale, west of Cork. Aguila's army of 3400 men was too small to fight Mountjoy on its own, and Tyrone and O'Donnell left the security of Ulster to aid the Spanish. Mountjoy managed to defeat the Spanish, even with the Irish help, a disaster for Tyrone's cause. Within a year Mountjoy had finally crushed the rebellion. At the end of March 1603 Tyrone made his submission to Elizabeth, unaware that the elderly Queen had died only days earlier. The Irish rebellion was over, but the costs to both Ireland and England were great.

The wars of the last 15 years of Elizabeth's reign had taken their toll both financially and in the number of men who were conscripted. Between 1558 and 1603 over 105 000 men served in the army. The total cost of war in those years, including the defeat of the Spanish Armada, was £4 500 000. Nearly £2 000 000 was spent on Ireland alone. By the last year of Elizabeth's reign, the Crown was having trouble paying its bills. The constant requests for money and men caused great resentment among the people. The last years of Elizabeth's reign were made more painful by the Earl of Esssex's unsuccessful rebellion against her in 1601. This rebellion was the last in a series of plots and conspiracies, attempts to assassinate the Queen or topple her regime in favor of someone else. Elizabeth's government not only had to deal with the strains of foreign policy, but with the question of the succession, which may have been the most sustained issue of her reign.

5

PLOTS, CONSPIRACIES, AND THE SUCCESSION[1]

The rebellion led by the desperate Earl of Essex in 1601 was only the last in a series of plots and conspiracies against Elizabeth that had punctuated the reign. Elizabeth always claimed that she ruled with the love of her subjects and Elizabeth was for the most part a well-loved and popular Queen. A discussion of the plots and attempts against her should not suggest that most of the English people wanted Elizabeth off the throne or dead; in fact, they rallied loyally around her and were infuriated by the conspiracies against their Queen. When they heard about Dr William Parry's plan to murder Elizabeth in 1585, members of Parliament tried to conceive of an even more horrible death sentence for him than the usual punishment of being hanged, drawn, and quartered. But her Council and Parliament were also well aware of the dangers that could surround Elizabeth, that Catholics could see Elizabeth as a target who, once she was out of way, would allow England to be restored to the true faith. Members of Parliament, especially once word was out about the plots to assassinate Elizabeth and place Mary Stuart on the throne, were vehement about the need to protect the Queen; they passed the Queen's Safety Act and signed a Bond of Association binding them to kill Mary Stuart should an assassin murder their Queen. Sir Francis Walsingham's web of spies did all it could to uncover plots and to destroy them. One of Elizabeth's closest advisors, William Cecil, Lord Burghley, was obsessed with worry about how to protect her and what would happen to England if anything should happen to its Queen. Many perceived Elizabeth's refusal to marry and have a child or name a successor as only exacerbating the situation; people were afraid of civil war and turmoil should the Queen die. But sometimes members of Elizabeth's government exaggerated the importance of some quite minor plots as a way to pressure the Queen or rally the people against the dangers of Catholicism or radical Protestanism. Some of these conspiracies were extremely dangerous; others may have been less so.

Guarding the Queen was difficult because of her own lack of concern about security. As Queen, Elizabeth was, at least theoretically, under the protection of three sets of guards.[2] The oldest set, the Seargeants-at-Arms, were numbered at 20, and by the time of Elizabeth's reign membership in this guard was an honorary post. The Yeoman of the Guard had been founded by Henry VII in 1485 and these were the actual guards of the palace. When Henry VIII became king in 1509 he also established a horse guard. Members of the horse guard were all well born. The best performers for her tilts were Yeoman; they escorted her to chapel and in public processions on foot. The position of Captain of the Guard was of high status; both Sir Christopher Hatton and Sir Walter Raleigh held it, and Raleigh claimed the position gave him more access to Elizabeth than he would have had as a member of the Privy Council. But the security for Elizabeth often left her vulnerable, largely because of her own refusal to take precautions. Burghley was deeply concerned about poison, not only of food, but about the possibility of poisoned gifts of perfumes or gloves. He wanted everything Elizabeth ate or drank to be tasted by someone else ahead of time, but often, especially when she was on progress, Elizabeth could not be bothered with these measures. The secret service that Burghley and Walsingham developed had few agents; its remarkable success was due to Walsingham's own instinct and hard work, and he constantly felt that Elizabeth never appreciated the range of the dangers against her.

Burghley was convinced that if Elizabeth were married with an heir, many of the assassination plots would stop since getting rid of Elizabeth would not end the royal house or the Protestant succession. But his attempts to convince the Queen to marry all ended in failure. The other option that her Council and Parliament wanted was for Elizabeth, at least until she did marry and have a child of her own, to name an heir and safeguard the succession. This, however, was something that Elizabeth absolutely refused to do. Her experiences as the heir in her sister Mary's reign, where she was the unwilling center of others' dissatisfaction and potential plots, warned Elizabeth what might happen were she to name an heir. She said she did not want someone else to be the rising sun while she was the setting sun. Rather than creating security, Elizabeth was convinced that a named heir provided the discontented with a focus for their intrigues. Indeed, the experiences in other European countries in the sixteenth century suggest there was merit to Elizabeth's point of view. In Spain in 1568 Philip II imprisoned his eldest son Don Carlos because he suspected his son was plotting against him; Don Carlos died in prison after six months, possibly from self-starvation. The same year Duke John of Finland not only toppled his brother Erik XIV of Sweden off the Swedish throne, he later had him poisoned. There was intense rivalry between Charles IX of France and his brother the Duke of Anjou. When Anjou became Henry III in 1574, the rivalry between him and his younger brother the Duke of Alençon, now Anjou, was so serious that Henry had his brother imprisoned at one point because of his intrigues. The potential heirs in England would also not have inspired confidence in Elizabeth. Yet her refusal to deal with the succession did cause great anxiety throughout the reign.

Only a few years after she became Queen in October 1562, the Council was in despair when Elizabeth was seriously ill with small-pox; everyone was convinced that she would die. The Council could not agree on an heir; some spoke for the Earl of Huntington, while others pressed the claims of Katherine Grey. Burghley suggested that the Council, along with others named by Elizabeth, would rule as a regency until Parliament could be called to settle the succession. The potential problems with this plan were immense, but even more problematic was Elizabeth's solution. When she thought she was dying, Elizabeth called her Council to her bedside and asked them to agree that Robert Dudley would be made Protector of the Realm with an annual income of £20 000. Elizabeth recovered. No doubt the members of the Council were relieved that they neither had to keep – nor break – that promise. We can understand why the Council would have considered Robert Dudley a dreadful prospect: both his father and his grandfather were executed as traitors, and many of them feared and disliked Robert himself. Elizabeth was ill again both in 1564 and 1572, causing great consternation over the succession. News of an assassination plot, or of the successful assassination of another Protestant leader, such as William of Orange in 1584, also caused terror. But there was no unanimity on other possible heirs, and anyone on whom Elizabeth settled the succession would have detractors. Other claimants and their followers would have been furious. Nor was this a prize she could award and then reverse her decision without terrible consequences.

In the first years of her reign the two strongest claimants were Mary Stuart and Katherine Grey. One other candidate some people found promising was Henry Hastings, Earl of Huntington, who owed his claim to his white rose Yorkist roots. His mother Catherine was the grand-daughter of Margaret, Countess of Salisbury, daughter of George, Duke of Clarence. Clarence had been the brother of Edward IV and of the last Plantagenet King, Richard III. By the 1560s a Yorkist title was highly problematic, but Huntington had support for a number of reasons, the most important one being that he was one of the few male claimants and Queens were still a new and worrisome phenomenon. Huntington was popular in his native Leicestershire and had support among the Puritans. He was also well connected at Court since his wife Catherine was Robert Dudley's sister. In the first years of the reign his name was often men-tioned and in the crisis of 1562 when the Council thought Elizabeth was dying some members advocated his claim, but after 1563 his importance as a claimant apparently declined. Huntington himself did nothing to promote it and he was not mentioned as a possibility in the 1566 Par-liament; Protestants instead rallied around Katherine Grey, who was closer in blood but highly problematic for other reasons.[3]

By right of primogeniture, the person with the best claim was Mary Stuart, granddaughter of Henry VIII's oldest sister Margaret by her first marriage to James IV of Scotland. Mary was the only surviving child of Margaret's son James V and thus, of course, was Queen of Scotland. But Mary was a foreigner and a Catholic, and indeed some Catholics claimed that she was already the rightful Queen since Elizabeth was illegitimate. This view made Mary seem a very dangerous heir to many Protestants in England. Mary Stuart was not, however, the only claimant descended from Margaret. After the death of James IV in 1513, Margaret had married Archibald Douglas, Earl of Angus, and they had had a daughter, also called Margaret, who had married Matthew, Earl of Lennox in 1544. They had two sons, Henry, Lord Darnley, the second husband of his cousin Mary Stuart, and Charles, who later in the reign married Elizabeth Cavendish. Mary and Darnley's son was James VI. Charles also had one child before his early death, a daughter Arbella. Since she was not born until 1575 Arbella was not a claimant early in the reign, though she was a potential heir at the end, and some hoped she might be an alternate heir to James VI. Some people questioned whether or not Margaret Lennox was legitimate, and thus could pass on her claim to the throne, as Angus had had the marriage to Margaret Tudor annulled on the basis of a precontract. In Scotland Margaret

Lennox was often openly referred to as a bastard and was not allowed to inherit from her father.

Also, Henry VIII's will specifically left out the descendents of his older sister Margaret in favor of his younger sister Mary, who had married Charles Brandon and had had two daughters who survived to have children of their own. The older daughter Frances had married Henry Grey, who eventually gained the title Duke of Suffolk, and they had had three daughters, Jane, Katherine, and Mary. There had, of course, already been an attempt to subvert the succession in favor of the eldest daughter Jane that had ended up costing both her and her father their lives, as well as the life of her young husband Guilford Dudley in 1554. The younger daughter Eleanor married Henry Clifford, afterwards second Earl of Cumberland. Their daughter Margaret married Henry Stanley, Lord Strange, afterwards Earl of Derby. Lady Margaret Strange argued that she would be an acceptable heir, but she had little support. She was married into an important Catholic family, which would negate Protestant interest, and Catholics had much stronger claimants elsewhere. Her claim, like Huntington's, was mentioned in the Parliament of 1563, but not 1566.

The swirl of claims and counter-claims was confused further by the fact that some argued that the marriage of Mary and Charles Brandon was not valid since he had been married previously and the dissolution of the marriage had been dubious. People wondered if Lady Margaret Mortimer was Charles Brandon's legal wife at the time he married Henry's widowed younger sister. If this were an invalid marriage, the daughters would be illegitimate and, again, ineligible to pass on their claim to the throne. A number of tracts written in the first decade of Elizabeth's reign argued this point. Not surprisingly, Protestant writers, such as John Hales, declared the marriage certainly valid while Catholic writers shed doubt on it.[4] Most of the claimants had dubious backgrounds of one sort or another. As Anne Somerset points out about the heirs at the beginning of the reign: "It was indeed a remarkable coincidence that with the exception of Mary Queen of Scots, every surviving descendant of Henry VII was marked to some extant by the stigma of illegitimacy."[5]

Early in the reign a number of claimants were mentioned as potential heirs. Within a few years the focus had narrowed to Mary Stuart or Katherine Grey. Elizabeth had always been wary of her Grey cousins and Katherine, who saw herself as a potential heir to the throne, was offended by the Queen's treatment in the first few months of Elizabeth's reign. But by the beginning of 1560, Elizabeth was showing her more favor, probably as a message to the French that Mary Stuart, then Queen Consort, was not the only potential heir. Whatever Elizabeth might have thought of Katherine Grey's claim, in her eyes Katherine clearly demonstrated her unfitness to rule by her secret marriage to Edward Seymour, Earl of Hertford. The Seymours had close ties with the Tudors: Hertford was the nephew of Henry's third wife and the son of the Lord Protector of Edward VI's reign. One might have thought what had happened to other members of their families (both fathers were executed as was Katherine's older sister Jane, who years before had been betrothed to Hertford) might have given them pause, but it did not. It seems to have truly been a love-match. In December 1560 the two eloped. Seymour's sister Jane arranged for the priest and stood witness. Seymour left the marriage certificate with his wife when he was sent to France on diplomatic business the following spring. The couple managed to keep the wedding a secret until that summer when Katherine found herself pregnant. She confided her plight to Robert Dudley, begging him to intercede for her with the Queen. Someone as close to the throne as Katherine making such a marriage without her consent outraged Elizabeth, and the Queen was even more disturbed when people claimed that the marriage only strengthened Katherine's right to succeed her.

Katherine was sent to the Tower, as was Seymour once he had been recalled from France. In September 1561 their son was born. Elizabeth was determined to demonstrate that theirs was not a legal marriage and an Ecclesiastical Commission was set to investigate. Unfortunately, Katherine had lost the documentation and, since Edward's sister Jane was dead and neither husband nor wife knew the name of the priest, they could provide no evidence that they had married.[6] The Commission ruled the marriage invalid, which meant their son was a bastard; both were sentenced to remain in the Tower to punish their unlawful copulation. But many people believed they were indeed husband and wife and that Elizabeth was unduly harsh toward the young couple. Though the two were imprisoned separately, a sympathetic jailer allowed them to visit each other; in February 1563 Katherine had a second son. Elizabeth made sure this would never happen again. Katherine was sent to live with her uncle Lord John Grey at Hammond in Middlesex under house arrest, and never saw her husband again. Norman Jones suggests that perhaps Elizabeth would have eventually forgiven Katherine and permitted her more freedom of movement, but in 1564 Member of Parliament John Hales published a pamphlet supporting Katherine's position as the heir. He challenged the findings of the Ecclesiastical Commission and proclaimed Katherine's sons as heirs to the throne. Elizabeth was as harsh to Hales as she had been to Katherine: after imprisonment in the Tower for a year, he was kept under house arrest until his death in 1571.[7] Hales outlived Katherine. Her constant weeping and refusal to eat may have shortened her life; she died of tuberculosis in 1568 at the age of 28.[8]

Though Elizabeth was troubled by Mary Stuart's position, in the early years of her reign she was more sympathetic to Mary's claim than she was to anyone else's. Certainly, the Scottish ambassador Maitland had this sense when he negotiated with Elizabeth over the succession and Mary's claim to the English throne in 1561. This did not, however, make her want to name Mary as her heir. Not only did she not trust her cousin, the struggle with Parliament over a Catholic heir would have been monumental. Mary's claim in the end caused Elizabeth far more lengthy and serious problems than those of the Suffolk branch.

Once Mary was widowed for the first time and had returned to Scotland, the question of her marriage had been paramount. Though in many ways Elizabeth narrowed Mary's choices to such an extent that Lord Darnley was one of the few options left, Mary's marriage to her cousin strengthened the Stuart claim, as did the birth of her son James. But it was only after Darnley's murder, her hasty marriage to Bothwell, the rebellion against her that led to her abdication, imprisonment, escape, and flight to England, that Mary's claim led to very serious problems of plots, rebellions, and conspiracies. Clearly, Elizabeth later regretted that she had threatened the Scots with retribution when some wanted to cut off the head of their errant Queen while they still had her in custody. Two decades later Elizabeth would be forced to do just that herself.

In May 1568 Mary escaped from Lochlevan, and mounted an army only to see it defeated in the field. Rather than wait for a ship that would take her to France, she crossed the border to England and took refuge at Carlisle Castle, placing herself at the mercy of her English cousin and fellow Queen. Elizabeth's first impulse was to be generous, but her Council was horrified to think of England supporting a Catholic Queen against their co-religionists in Scotland. Cecil suggested that Mary be kept in England and there be a public inquiry into the reasons for the rebellion against her. This could, he argued, give Mary the chance to clear herself of the suspicion that she had been involved in the murder of Lord Darnley. Both Mary and her half-brother Moray, the Regent, were invited to submit evidence to the commissioners Elizabeth appointed to hear the case. The commissioners were the Duke of Norfolk, the Earl of Sussex, and Sir Ralph Sadler. At first, Mary agreed to the procedure. She was moved to Bolton Castle in Yorkshire. Once Mary realized, however, that she had no freedom of movement, she asked to go to France. Elizabeth refused. In October 1568 representatives of both the Scottish lords and Mary appeared before Elizabeth's commissioners. Moray produced the Casket Letters, those highly disputed documents that if genuine, demonstrated Mary's guilt.[9] Mary asked to be allowed to appear before Elizabeth and the Privy Council to plead her case personally. But with Cecil's encouragement, Elizabeth refused to meet with Mary while she was still under suspicion, leading Mary's representatives led by John Leslie, Bishop of Ross, to withdraw from the proceedings. Elizabeth then ruled that since Mary had not presented her case, the commissioners could not judge the proceedings; Mary would be kept in restraint in England indefinitely until a better solution could be reached. Elizabeth was especially concerned because she heard rumors that the head of the commission – Norfolk – was interested in marrying the Scots Queen, who had obtained from the Pope an annulment of her marriage to Bothwell. Elizabeth warned Norfolk against such a match and he assured Elizabeth that he was not interested: he wanted, he claimed, to rest easy on his pillow at night, which he could not do if he were to marry someone whom he described as a murderer and adulterer. After such a conversation it would have been hard for him to admit that he continued to work to achieve the marriage.[10]

Elizabeth had become convinced that Mary was a threat to her security. Certainly, she found it disquieting that her chief commissioner Norfolk was secretly considering marrying Mary once she had obtained a divorce from Bothwell. Elizabeth's concern became much more intense the following year when England erupted into rebellion. One focus point for the northern rebellion was the Florentine banker Roberto Ridolfi (also spelled Ridolphi), who was living in London and eventually became an agent of the Pope. Another was the Spanish ambassador Guerau DeSpes, who in 1569 became involved in a conspiracy that had been developing among some of the older nobility in the north such as Norfolk, Thomas Percy, seventh Earl of Northumberland, and Charles Neville, sixth Earl of Westmoreland. Some of the great established families in the north perceived themselves more as petty sovereigns than as subjects. When Elizabeth had become Queen she had attempted to weaken her over-mighty subjects by transferring important offices out of their hands and instead appointing both "new men" she could trust from the south and lesser northerners who lacked a strong independent power base. As Christopher Haigh points out, while this strategy may have moved some of the magnates toward rebellion, it also meant that in 1569 the government in the north remained intact and overcame the rising.[11] As much of a crisis as the rising in the north seemed to Elizabeth and her government, its lack of success is an important statement of the success of her rule.

While some of the grievances and concerns of the northern nobility differed, they were united in their distrust of Cecil and the direction of Elizabeth's government. For a while, a number of the old nobility had been upset over the new men in government gaining power and prestige, which they saw as going hand in hand with a growing estrangement with Spain and ecclesiastical innovations. They disliked the way Mary Stuart had been treated. They wanted the succession settled on her and, in the meantime, her restoration as Queen of Scotland. Cecil would be pushed out of power and Elizabeth would rule under the control and direction of the old nobility. For DeSpes this was not the goal: he wanted Elizabeth off the throne and Mary Queen of a restored Catholic England. The Earls of Northumberland and Westmoreland, whatever their published statements during the northern rebellion, were also sympathetic to this scenario.

The plot against Cecil by Norfolk and Arundel and some of the other nobility disintegrated as Elizabeth demonstrated her support for him. But the concern over what to do about Mary Stuart and her claim to the English throne continued to be a problem. Cecil was more and more convinced that Mary was an enemy of Elizabeth's and Protestant England, and that the Scottish Queen would not rest until she had replaced Elizabeth on the throne and restored Catholicism. Yet if Elizabeth died, Mary's claim was extremely strong. While Cecil and his allies wanted to keep Mary in confinement and unacknowledged as heir, a number of courtiers who were less zealously Protestant, including Leicester, were convinced that, to protect their position and the Protestant religion should Elizabeth predecease Mary, the best hope would be for Mary to marry an English nobleman who would control her. In the meantime, they wanted her restored as Queen of Scotland and so out of England. The Duke of Norfolk seemed the best choice as he was of high birth but not so powerful as to be feared and had been committed to the idea of marrying Mary since the beginning of 1569. But Moray and his supporters in Scotland did not want Mary back and Elizabeth did not want to name Mary heir. In September 1569 Leicester broke the news of the negotiations of the projected Norfolk-Mary Stuart marriage to Elizabeth and she clearly forbade it. She forgave Leicester for any part in the plan and the other Protestant lords immediately abandoned the idea. Elizabeth also severely warned Norfolk, who now felt isolated, especially as his friends Pembroke and Arundel were conveniently away from court.

The Catholic lords planned to force Elizabeth to agree to the marriage of Mary and Norfolk and restore them to their ancient privileges. For DeSpes, it was more. He wanted Elizabeth off the throne with Spanish help. But Alva had told Philip months before that he had neither the money nor the ships for an invasion and any attempt to help Mary Stuart would lead to a disastrous war. Spain officially warned DeSpes to stop his involvement in plots with Mary Stuart's servants. In the fall of 1569 the northern lords were on their own, though they still hoped for aid from Spain.

But Norfolk's relations with the treasonable wing of the opposition had its problems also. In May 1569 his six-year-old step-son and ward Lord Dacre was accidentally killed when he tried to vault over a rickety wooden horse. Norfolk immediately claimed the extensive Dacre lands in Cumberland, Westmoreland, and Yorkshire for the boy's three sisters, who were his wards and whom he planned to marry to his sons. But this claim was contested by the girls' uncle, Leonard Dacre, a leading northern Catholic. Dacre was an ardent Catholic and strong supporter of Mary Stuart. But now the two men were enemies.[12] Still, Westmoreland was married to Norfolk's sister, and though neither he nor Northumberland seem to have thought very highly of Norfolk, they had enough grievances of their own to join him in his marriage scheme, even with Dacre's legal battles with Norfolk. But the relationship between the Court conspirators and the northern Earls was always problematic. Northumberland had been Mary's biggest supporter since she had come into England and had looked for Spanish support for her.

Norfolk withdrew from Court without taking leave of the Queen. On route to his country home he planned to visit his supporter the Earl of Pembroke. While traveling, a servant of Arundel warned him that the conspirators were in danger. He stopped at Howard House in London to secretly consult with Mary's emissary John Leslie, the Bishop of Ross, who demanded that Mary needed to know what he would do now that Elizabeth disapproved of the marriage. Mary pressed Norfolk to release her by force of arms. But Norfolk feared he would be sent to the Tower for what he had done and fled to his country house, taking to his bed in illness. The rebellion was supposed to begin when Norfolk left Court in September for his country house at Kenninghall in East Anglia.

At Kenninghall, fearful of what would be done to him, Norfolk wrote to Elizabeth begging pardon and to his fellows conspirators telling them not to go ahead or his life might be forfeit. Norfolk may have been aware that the Earls of Pembroke and Arundel were already under detention at Court and that others were being watched. Elizabeth summoned him back to Court and on his way he was intercepted and lodged in the Tower. When the northern Earls heard on 10 October about Norfolk's imprisonment, they met the next day at Northumberland's house in Yorkshire. Westmoreland was convinced that they should mobilize their retainers for their own protection and convinced Northumberland. Northumberland sent word to DeSpes that Norfolk's weakness had ruined the entire plot.

At the same time, Elizabeth sent word to the Earl of Sussex, Lord President of the Council at York, that he should warn all Justices of the Peace throughout the north that they should keep good watch. Sussex obtained assurances from the two Earls that all was quiet and that the problems were just rumors. He let the Queen know this, but she was still very concerned, and on 24 October instructed Sussex to order the Earls to come to Court immediately. Sussex remonstrated with Elizabeth, telling the Queen this would only drive them into rebellion. But Elizabeth insisted. On 12 November both Earls were at Brancepeth, Westmoreland's castle, and they had their followers armed and ready. Dacre was away at Court in the midst of his litigation against Norfolk and his absence from the north deprived them of an important ally.

Sussex responded by ordering a general mobilization of the armed forces in the north and issued a proclamation denouncing the treason of the Earls, but he still made a last attempt to recall the Earls to their duty. He wrote on 13 November that their friends would intercede for them with Elizabeth, whom he described as someone who never took extreme positions and who always had affection for the Earls. It was too late; the Earls marched, they claimed, for the true religion and against false councillors. On 14 November the rebels entered Durham. In the cathedral they celebrated the mass in Latin and trampled underfoot the Anglican Prayer Book and English Bibles. Sussex had trouble getting the north to rouse to its own defense and urgently appealed to the government for help. The Justices of the Peace and the gentlemen of the north were mostly holding aloof, though not actively supporting the rebels. But a number of frontier posts had been given to men loyal to Elizabeth and they held them in the Queen's name. Berwick was in the hands of Lord Hunsdon, Elizabeth's cousin.

The Earls published a proclamation claiming their hostility was not to the Queen but against her evil councillors who had overthrown the Catholic religion, dishonored the realm and attempted to destroy the nobility. They wished for ancient customs and liberties to be restored. The rebels moved south to try to free Mary Stuart, and Elizabeth ordered her moved to Coventry and had a great concentration of royal troops in Lincolnshire, Leicestershire, and Warwickshire. The rebels retreated back to the north, with Sussex and the reinforcements led by Lord Hunsdon in pursuit. They reached Durham on 15 December and realized their position was hopeless. They disbanded their foot soldiers and headed to Scotland. Once at the Scottish borders, staunch Catholics there gave hospitality to the fugitives. The Scottish Regent Moray, however, captured Northumberland and had him taken to Edinburgh. But Moray was assassinated in late January, and it took two years and considerable money before the Scots gave up Northumberland to be executed by the English. Westmoreland fled to a life of exile in Flanders.

Lord Dacre was convinced that Elizabeth would blame him for the escape of the rebels and formed an alliance with the Scots. Elizabeth told Lord Hunsdon to arrest Dacre as an army was being mounted in Scotland. In February 1570 Hunsdon defeated Dacre's forces before the reinforcements arrived. In the meantime the southern army was despoiling the north, though Sussex did all he could to stop it. By 4 February 500 of the rebels, mostly poorer men without influence, had been executed by martial law as an example. Elizabeth then sent word to let people off with fines if they promised submission. Elizabeth was merciful to Pembroke, Arundel, and Lumley. Though some had doubted Sussex's loyalty given his friendship with Norfolk, he had worked hard and loyally to defeat the Queen's enemies and was subsequently named a Privy Councillor. The northern rebellion had been a real and frightening crisis, but the victory of the Crown was clear and regional politics were giving way to national loyalty. Foreign support did not materialize, and though the Pope took the opportunity to support the rebels by excommunicating Elizabeth, the bull of excommunication came too late to have any effect. Tudor authority became stronger in the north and Cecil emerged from these crises in a stronger position than ever. In the summer of 1570 Elizabeth still hoped there would be some way to send Mary back to Scotland as a Queen with only nominal power and she was attempting to negotiate with the Scots who had little interest in such a scheme.

In August 1570 Norfolk was allowed to leave the Tower for Howard House in London, though he was still under some constraint. He signed a submission binding himself to give up any idea of marriage with Mary Stuart or involvement in her cause. But Norfolk still dreamed of a royal marriage. He had the submission shown to Mary before he signed it and continued to correspond with her afterwards. Ridolfi had been examined by Walsingham, but had managed to convince him and Cecil that he was not involved. The northern rebellion had failed, but the papal agent Ridolfi and the Spanish ambassador DeSpes, working with the Bishop of Ross, thought that there could still be a rising that – with foreign Catholic help – would place Mary Stuart on the English throne.

The Ridolfi Plot[13], as it came to be known, evolved into a plan where Alva would send over money and men. The force would march on London, while the Duke of Norfolk and his friends would rise in revolt. Catholicism would be restored to England as Mary and Norfolk ruled as King and Queen of both England and Scotland. At the end of March 1571 Ridolfi left England for a series of meetings with the Duke of Alva, Philip II, and the Pope. While Alva was again unimpressed with the idea of an invasion and considered Ridolfi a "windbag and fool,"[14] Ridolfi got a better reception in both Madrid and Rome. Philip promised that if Elizabeth were assassinated, Alva would lead an invasion. Ridolfi foolishly sent back word to his conspirators in England that the plans were going well, but his messenger Charles Bailly was arrested when he returned to England and was found to have with him incriminating letters from Ridolfi to the Bishop of Ross. Bailly eventually made a full confession, giving Burghley some aspects of the plot. In August further plotting was discovered when Norfolk was found to be sending £600 to Mary's supporters in Scotland. His servants were arrested and his house searched, which presented Elizabeth's government with the entire plot. The Bishop of Ross was arrested and soon made a full confession that was damning to Norfolk. DeSpes was expelled from England in January 1572. The same month Norfolk was tried before his peers at Westminster and found guilty of treason. But Elizabeth was reluctant to execute Norfolk; they were related by blood and he was the only duke in the realm. Three times she signed his death warrant and then had it recalled.

If Elizabeth had been wary of Mary before, she was now furious with her, as Mary's complicity in the plot was demonstrable. Mary had foolishly fully committed herself to paper and these letters eventually got into the government's hands. Ridolfi's messenger had been arrested shortly after Elizabeth had sent commissioners to Scotland to negotiate her return as Queen, though with limited power. But when Elizabeth learned of Mary's own involvement in the plot, she abandoned the policy of restoration or liberty for Mary under any circumstances. She also agreed with Cecil on the value of publicly damaging Mary's reputation. George Buchanan's *Detection* – the story of Mary, Darnley, and Bothwell from the point of view of the Scottish Protestant lords – was translated and published together with the Casket Letters. When Parliament met that May, the House of Commons insisted not only on Norfolk's execution but Mary's as well, calling for Elizabeth to cut off her cousin's head and make no more ado about it. While Elizabeth refused to have an anointed Queen executed, Norfolk was beheaded that June; he was, however, the only one to suffer.

Protestants in England were not only outraged, but deeply worried in the summer of 1572, a feeling which intensified with the St Bartholomew's Day massacre that August. If Elizabeth were assassinated, as Moray had been in 1570 in Scotland and as Coligny had been in France, religious wars would engulf England as well. Walsingham, as Secretary of State, saw it as his mission to make sure that Mary was well guarded and could not plan for Elizabeth's assassination and her own freedom. Mary was the "guest" of George Talbot, the Earl of Shrewsbury, who was ordered to watch her closely. After the Ridolfi Plot, Walsingham was aware that Mary was again attempting to secretly communicate with her supporters, but for a while was unable to stop the flow. He finally got information from Scotland that led to the arrest of Henry Cockyn, a stationer and bookseller in London whose shop had been used as the center point for incoming and outgoing mail. It appeared that some of the Earl of Shrewsbury's servants, including his one-time secretary Thomas Morgan, were involved. A number of them were arrested and imprisoned for some months, though Morgan, warned of his impending arrest, fled to Paris where he continued to work for Mary's cause.[15] Throughout the 1570s Walsingham was hearing about plans to murder Elizabeth, free Mary, and marry her off to some convenient, powerful Catholic. The ambassador who replaced DeSpes, Bernardino de Mendoza, who reopened the Spanish embassy in 1578, equally saw his mission as working to bring England back to the Catholic faith. Mendoza became convinced even before he convinced his master Philip II that it was no longer possible or even desirable for Spain to coexist peaceably with Protestant England, and that he, as ambassador, should do anything he could to destroy Elizabeth and her government.[16]

The plots of the latter 1570s did not come to anything, but in 1582 Walsingham learned about a much more potentially serious conspiracy with Mary herself at the center. Francis Throckmorton, the Catholic nephew of Sir Nicholas Throckmorton, after being educated at Oxford, went on a prolonged tour of the Continent where he met exiled English Catholics and was drawn into a plot with both France and Spain. The plan was for the Duke of Guise, with the financial support of Pope Gregory XIII and Philip II, to invade England. Mary Stuart's agent in Paris, Thomas Morgan, put Throckmorton in touch with Mendoza in London, who was working with two Jesuits, the Englishman William Holt and William Creighton, a Scotsman. They had been sent to Scotland to work with Catholic allies there. In 1583 Throckmorton took a house in London which was the center of communication between Morgan in Paris, Mendoza, and Mary Stuart, with whom Throckmorton corresponded directly. Walsingham intercepted some of Mary's secret correspondence and learned of Throckmorton's involvement. For six months Walsingham had Throckmorton watched, finally deciding to arrest him in November 1583.

While he was able to destroy one letter to Mary and get a dangerous cache of documents from Mendoza safely away before his arrest, what was found in his house was still damning, including a list of the Catholic nobles and gentlemen willing to support an invasion and the safe places where foreign armies could land. After being racked, Throckmorton confessed everything. He was convicted of treason and executed in July 1584. Mendoza was so deeply involved in the conspiracy that in January 1584 the Council called him before them and gave him 15 days to get out of England. He was the last resident Spanish ambassador of Elizabeth's reign and dedicated the rest of his career to plotting against her. Creighton was captured by the Dutch, who returned him to England. After two years in the Tower he was released, but continued to conspire aganst Elizabeth; he eventually died in France. James VI imprisoned Holt and refused to return him to Elizabeth, eventually allowing him to escape. Holt would also continue to conspire against the Queen until his death in 1599. Thomas Morgan, still in Paris, almost immediately got involved in another plot, this time with Dr William Parry and Edmund Neville. Parry, an obscure family connection of Burghley's who had sat in Parliament, was deeply in debt and this may have been his motivation. Neville was a cousin of the exiled rebel, Westmoreland. Parry told Neville he planned to assassinate Elizabeth in the Palace Gardens. Though Parry was able to approach her, he lost his nerve and both he and Neville ended up in the Tower. Parry claimed he was acting as an *agent provocateur* and had no intention of harming the Queen, but this excuse was not accepted. He was executed in March 1585; Neville was released from the Tower ten years later.[17]

Throckmorton's conspiracy and Parry's plot alarmed the English, as did the wild plan of a young Warwickshire Catholic gentleman named John Somerville, or Somerfield. In the summer of 1583 he became convinced that he was chosen to save Catholics from persecution and headed to London, assaulting people on the way and making no secret of his plan to kill Elizabeth and put her head on a pole. He was soon arrested and implicated his wife and several friends, all of whom were arrested. Somerville pleaded guilty, but the others all swore they knew nothing about it. While all were found guilty and condemned to die, only Somerville and one friend were executed; the others were pardoned. Somerville was not part of any well-organized plot, but a single madman could be an effective assassin – if Elizabeth were killed the whole structure of the Elizabethan government would have been immediately destroyed – and the presumptive heir to the throne was still Mary Stuart. No one could even legally avenge Elizabeth's murder, since all royal officials would lose their commissions at the death of the monarch.

In the fall of 1584 Walsingham and Burghley decided they must deal with this danger and drafted the Bond of Association. Each subsequent draft of the Bond became more violent and it reflected the deep fears of the Protestant English political nation at the time. The first clause of the Bond bound all who signed it to obey the Queen and to pursue and exterminate any who attempted to harm her. The next clause, however, was crucial. In its final wording, the Bond pledged its signatories that in the event of an attempt on Elizabeth's life, it would not only bar from the succession the person for whom the attempt was made, but the members of the Bond would also kill that person by whatever means necessary. Mary Stuart was not mentioned by name, but she did not need to be: all knew it was aimed directly at her. Though the wording was ambiguous, some also believed that it was aimed not only at the claimant, but also at the claimant's heir – James VI, if he were to claim the English throne, would also be hunted down. Since the Pope had sanctioned Elizabeth's assassination, the Protestants would also answer violence with violence. David Cressy calls the Bond "a masterly piece of propaganda ... a dramatic and public attestation of loyalty to Queen Elizabeth."[18] Copies of the Bond were sent all over England, strongly encouraging loyal Englishmen to join the Association if they wished and, in fact, thousands did so, though some were appalled by the lawlessness of the Bond and refused to sign it.

When Parliament met in late 1584, enacting legislation to provide for Elizabeth's defense was also their most pressing concern. In December

1584 a bill for the Queen's safety, inspired by the Bond of Association, was debated in the House of Commons. The Queen's Safety Act dealt specifically with anyone making an attempt on the Queen's life in order to advance a claimant to the throne. The Act authorized people to pursue and kill both culprits and claimants, an echo of the Bond of Association. The Act differed from the Bond, however, in stating that the claimant's heirs were not included, and that the Queen would be able to restore the title of the heir if she saw fit. The Act was thoroughly aimed at Mary Stuart, but her son James was potentially exempt. There was a great deal of debate in committee over the Act. Some members were particularly concerned over the problem of, if the Queen were actually killed and all authority lapsed, how effective action could be taken. Clearly, members were not united on the bill.

Elizabeth then intervened. On 18 December Sir Christopher Hatton informed members that while the Queen greatly appreciated their care in her protection, she believed her safety was in God's hands; she could not consent that anyone should be punished for the fault of another. She especially did not wish the penalties to extend to the offender's issue – obviously James VI – unless he were also at fault. The committee met that afternoon to revise the bill, but this caused further dissention and Elizabeth's own misgivings caused her to decide to delay; the bill was to be shelved until after the Christmas recess.

During the recess Burghley worked hard to transform the bill into a measure that would be both effective and acceptable. He proposed a bill which would provide, in the event of Elizabeth's murder, that all officials would continue in office "in the name of the Crown of England," and an executive body, a "Grand Council," would temporarily have the authority to govern the realm until those who had been concerned with the Queen's death were indicted, tried, and executed. A Parliament would be called to determine all claims to the Crown. This plan, however, was never placed before the House of Commons because Elizabeth refused to accept it. When Parliament met in February, the committee, in a deadlock, asked the Queen's advice about what they should do. Burghley then drafted a new bill in consultation with Elizabeth and Hatton introduced the bill into the House of Commons for a first reading. The text of the bill was based on the earlier one, but also took into account Elizabeth's concerns. In the event of a rebellion, invasion, or plot against the Queen there would be a set of commissioners to investigate and pronounce judgement. All subjects would pursue to the death anyone the commission declared had known about the offense. Were the Queen actually killed, only those for whom the assassination was effected were to be killed, not their heirs unless they also were involved. If Elizabeth were assassinated, Mary Stuart would suffer for it, but not James. Instead of Burghley's plan, the commission was solely to investigate and destroy the guilty. Parliament passed this version of the Queen's Safety Act and the Bond of Association was amended to conform with it.

While the Bond of Association and the Queen's Safety Act put potential assassins on warning, these measures were not enough in themselves to protect the Queen. Walsingham had been appalled at how easily Mary had been able to correspond secretly while in the guardianship of the Earl of Shrewsbury. In 1585 she was transferred to the keeping of Walsingham's trusted friend, Sir Amyas Paulet, a Puritan. At Chartley manor house, Paulet treated Mary with respect; she was not, however, able to charm him. Walsingham insisted that Mary and her retinue be effectively isolated from the outside world while she was in Paulet's care. But Walsingham wanted Mary to think that she could still secretly communicate and he began an operation that would end in her death.

In December 1585 the Catholic exile Gilbert Gifford came over from France. Thomas Morgan had given him the job of finding a way of evading Paulet's vigilance and securing a line of communication with Mary. Gifford had had a checkered career as a Catholic abroad and it is possible that while at Rheims in Cardinal Willliam Allen's seminary, he was actually spying for Walsingham. In October 1585 he moved on to Paris and thence to England. He was arrested as soon as he landed and brought to Walsingham. Certainly, from that time on, he was a double agent. Gifford, Walsingham, and Walsingham's assistant Thomas Phelippes developed a plan where secret letters could be smuggled in and out of Chartley in the false bottoms of beer barrels. Mary and her supporters would think that Gifford had developed a safe means of communication. Phelippes was an expert linguist and brilliant at breaking codes so that Walsingham was able to read all that went in and out of Chartley. Thus when the Babington plot was hatched, Walsingham was in on it from the beginning.

It was a familiar kind of plan: a rising of English Catholics, aided by an invading army; release of Mary; murder of Elizabeth; restoration of Catholicism. Mendoza, now based in Paris, and Thomas Morgan were also involved from the start, as was the priest John Ballard, the go-between who represented the English Catholics. Walsingham got one of his spies accepted by Ballard, who then accompanied him as they traveled back and forth across the Channel. Ballard approached Anthony

Babington since Babington was known to be one of Mary's strongest supporters. Anthony Babington, yet another young man in Mary's cause whose enthusiasm was greater than his abilities, came from a wealthy Derbyshire family and had met Mary when he had been a page in the Earl of Shrewsbury's household. Ballard asked Babington to accept the task of murdering Elizabeth. Babington and Mary began to correspond and Babington assured Mary he had six friends who so supported her and the Catholic cause they would join together in the execution of the Queen. Mary responded in such explicit detail that Walsingham had more than enough to demonstrate her complicity. But he wanted to know the names of Babington's friends and had Phelippes forge a postscript to Mary's response asking Babington for his friends' names, which he willingly supplied. Early August 1586 Walsingham was ready to round up the conspirators, including Ballard, Babington, and his friends. Amyas Paulet took Mary out for a stag hunt with her two secretaries; outside, the secretaries were arrested and Mary then placed in confinement while her rooms at Chartley were searched and her confidential papers confiscated. The evidence was more than enough to guarantee that Mary would be found guilty when put on trial.

Elizabeth was outraged by the Babington conspiracy and considered hanging, drawing, and quartering too merciful for Babington and his friends, though Burghley assured her that if done properly it would be exceedingly painful. The usual practice was for the executioner to hang the prisoner until he was dead and do the gruesome rest of the punishment to the lifeless body, but for Babington and three of his confederates, the execution was as prolonged and excruciating as possible. When it was described to Elizabeth she had a sudden change of heart and the other conspirators were allowed to hang until their death. But it was one thing to try and execute, however painfully, her own subjects and quite another to put on trial and execute a fellow Queen. Elizabeth was extremely reluctant to do so.

Foreign supporters of Mary were also mobilizing diplomatic support. Henry III of France warned Elizabeth he would deeply resent the trial and execution of Mary, once Queen Consort of France herself. Though years before the Scots had wanted Mary returned so that they could execute her themselves, now they were outraged that Elizabeth might do so. While Elizabeth no longer was opposed to Mary's death, she did not want the precedent of a monarch – or former monarch – subject to trial and execution. She would have greatly preferred if one of her loyal subjects – so many, after all, had signed the Bond of Association – would surreptitiously murder Mary. But Walsingham and Burghley wanted Mary publicly tried and convinced the rest of the Council that this was in England's best interest. Puritan members of Parliament also pressured Elizabeth for Mary's trial and execution.

Elizabeth did not want Mary lodged in the Tower or to have the trial in London; after much wavering, she finally agreed to appoint commissioners to hold a trial at Fotheringhay Castle in Northamptonshire in mid-October. But the day before the trial was to begin, Elizabeth sent word that though the commissioners could proceed with the trial, they could not pronounce verdict or sentence. Mary denied her guilt as well as objecting to being tried at all, but the evidence against her included a copy of her letter to Babington and the confession of her two secretaries. At the end of the second day, when the evidence was complete, the presiding judge, Lord Chancellor Sir Thomas Bromley, announced that both judgement and sentence would be reserved. Delaying judgement only increased the pressure from both sides on Elizabeth. While the Privy Council was urging Elizabeth to go forward, the French ambassador brought a strongly worded message from his King that stated Mary's execution would outrage all Christian rulers. But such a remark only angered Elizabeth, who agreed that the commissioners could pass judgement. Parliament continued to clamor for the Scots Queen's death, but Elizabeth was still reluctant to actually allow Mary's execution and postponed signing the death warrant. She finally signed it in February 1587 and Mary was executed, but Elizabeth claimed that the warrant was dispatched without her knowledge or consent. The Queen publicly expressed her grief and anger over the execution; William Davison, Principal Secretary, was imprisoned in the Tower where she threatened him with execution. Davison was finally quietly released and his fine remitted though he was never employed in the Queen's service again. People at the time, and historians later, have debated just how upset Elizabeth really was; perhaps she did not know herself. She was correct, however, that it was a dangerous precedent: Mary's grandson and Elizabeth's next successor but one, Charles I, was also tried, convicted, and beheaded in the middle of the next century.

Mary's execution in 1587 and the defeat of the Spanish Armada the following year did not end the plots against Elizabeth's life, though the ones of the 1590s did not have the same organization or, probably, the same degree of danger. Some, indeed, may well have been greatly exaggerated or even fabricated to gain political favor or whip up popular hysteria. Certainly, that was one element of the denouncement by the

Earl of Essex in 1594 of Elizabeth's Christianized Jewish physician, Dr Roderigo Lopez, for a plot to poison the Queen; that incident will be discussed in depth in the next chapter. The government was still deeply worried about Spain and Catholic plots on the one side, and furious over the embarrassment caused by radical Protestants on the other. The 1591 case of William Hacket was manipulated by the government as a way to embarrass the Puritan Thomas Cartwright, even though he was not involved with Hacket. The government was upset by Cartwright and the Puritan movement, and nine Puritan ministers were at the time being tried before the Star Chamber. Often the government disregarded those they considered "brain sick lunatics," but if there was political threat or political gain to be made of them the position was very different.[19]

William Hacket had been whipped out of York for proclaiming himself a second John the Baptist. When he got to London, he promoted himself to Jesus Christ and King of Europe. He would pray out in the streets with great theatricality, as if he were speaking to God face to face. Two young men of Puritan leanings, Edmund Copinger and Henry Arthington, met Hacket in May 1591. Copinger was a Puritan sympathizer and very upset with the trial of the nine ministers. In July the two young men went into the streets telling passersby to "repent, England, repent," and proclaimed Hacket Messiah and King and Elizabeth no longer Queen. Copinger's harangues caused a riot and the three were arrested and put on trial. Hacket was found guilty of attempting to deprive Elizabeth of her title and was executed. Copinger starved himself to death in prison or so it was said; Arthington was released after writing a suitably apologetic narrative. Though it was tenuous, the government did all it could to link Copinger to Cartwright and publicized the case as much as possible. Some people at the time wondered, and historians today still wonder, if the government took the Hacket case much too seriously, but it proved a politically valuable way to undercut the Puritan movement.

Some historians also question the seriousness of Edward Squire's assassination attempt of Elizabeth and the Earl of Essex in 1598 as well. Squire, though he had been able to gain some education, had had a job in Elizabeth's stables. Unhappy with that position, he had signed up to sail with Francis Drake in 1595 on what would be Drake's last voyage to the West Indies. The ship that Squire was on got separated from the rest and was captured by the Spanish. Squire apparently offered his services to the English Jesuit Father Richard Walpole and Squire was returned to England in June 1597, under orders to poison Elizabeth and the Earl of Essex. He was paid in advance for his services. Squire obtained his old job in the Queen's stable and rubbed some poison on Elizabeth's saddle and pommel, but with no result. A week or so later, in part to avoid detection and also perhaps so that he could make his attempt on Essex's life, he signed up to set sail with Essex. While at sea, he rubbed poison on the Earl's chair with the same singular lack of success. Rather than recognizing that poor Squire, sometimes referred to as "the pathetic assassin," was simply a failure at all he tried to accomplish, his masters in Spain came to believe that Squire might be a double agent. Upset that he had taken money and not performed for it, someone informed the English government about Squire's attempts at political assassination. Squire was arrested and in November 1598 indicted for high treason. He was repeatedly examined and, probably under torture, confessed the whole sorry affair. The government made the most of his trial to demonstrate the evil nature of Spain and the Jesuits, and Squire was executed. Pamphlets by government officials about both Hacket and Squire furthered the propaganda value of the cases, while exiled Catholics claimed it was all invented to discredit them.[20]

Possibly, both the Hacket and the Squire case were exaggerated by a worried government to discredit Puritans or Catholics. But the government took the rebellion led by the Earl of Essex in 1601 very seriously indeed. Essex's 1599 return from Ireland without her permission and the disastrous Irish campaign had greatly angered Elizabeth. She had him confined to his house while he was under investigation. Though not tried before the Star Chamber, Essex was brought to trial at York House in June 1600. While he was cleared of disloyalty to the Queen, he was found guilty of misgoverance in Ireland and was suspended from his offices and ordered to remain a prisoner, still under house arrest, during the Queen's pleasure. By the end of August 1600 Essex could move about freely, though he could not return to Court. Essex continued to besiege Elizabeth with letters asking to be returned to favor, but he also considered what to do if she refused. He was deeply in debt; simply retiring to private life was not an option he accepted. In November 1600 Elizabeth refused to renew his monopoly on sweet wines, which was a financial disaster for Essex. His behavior became far more wild and uncontrolled after this disappointment, as did his language. He said of Elizabeth that her conditions were as crooked as her carcass. Raleigh was convinced that this statement, which was repeated to Elizabeth, hurt Essex's credit more than anything. His more responsible followers ceased to have any involvement with him, and Essex House became a focal point for adventurers who were dissatisfied with Elizabeth and her government. Essex persuaded himself that he might be treacherously murdered by Raleigh or Robert Cecil. The inner core of the conspiracy met at Drury House, the lodging of Henry Wriothesley, Earl of Southampton, at the beginning of February 1601. In an attempt to avoid suspicion, Essex himself did not attend. They discussed Essex's plan to seize the Court and force Elizabeth to change the leaders of her government, especially Robert Cecil, even if this meant doing violence to the Queen's person.

But the Court was hearing rumors. On 8 February Lord Keeper Thomas Egerton and three others came to Essex House with an order from the Queen that Essex come at once to Court. Essex refused and had them kept under constraint. It was obviously hopeless to try to surprise the Court so Essex turned instead to the city of London. With his supporters, who numbered less than 200, Essex marched through London expecting the populace to throng out to join him. Meanwhile, Robert Cecil sent a warning to the Mayor and heralds, which denounced Essex as a traitor in the streets. None of the citizens joined him and most of his supporters melted away. Essex, desperate, bolted back to Essex House, where those he had left in charge had freed the hostages in hopes of clemency. A force led by Lord Admiral Charles Howard besieged the house, and by evening Essex had surrendered. Less than two weeks after the aborted rebellion, he was tried and found guilty of treason.

There was no wide-scale retribution. Essex himself and four others were executed. Otherwise, Elizabeth treated the rebels with great leniency, letting most of them off with fines. Southampton, though condemned, was reprieved; he was freed from the Tower on the accession of James. Though Essex had been a great popular hero, the city of London had refused to support him and had stayed loyal to the end to their Queen, but the rebels were the extreme representation of a great deal of discontent at the end of the reign. Essex's death was hard on both Elizabeth and her popularity. Eighteen months after his execution, a German visitor reported that all he heard sung in the streets of the city was "Essex's Last Goodnight." At Court, people saw how much Elizabeth had aged since the Essex rebellion, that she sat in the dark and wept for the dead young Earl.

After all the worry about the succession, when Elizabeth died in March 1603, there was a smooth transition to her cousin James VI of Scotland, Mary Stuart's son. Despite the range of possible successors at the end of the reign as at the beginning, there was a clear and general consensus for James. Though it is probable that the accounts that she named James as her heir on her deathbed were fabricated after her death, she had been right when she had told her people not to worry about the succession. Elizabeth had been right, but England had been lucky – had she died in the first decade, had any of the assassination plots been successful, England may well have been plunged into civil war. The transition was smooth, but England in the last decade of Elizabeth's reign was going through a lot of changes; there were great cultural achievements, but also some grave difficulties. The final chapter will examine issues of diversity and change as the century and Elizabeth's reign were ending.

6
CULTURE AND DIFFERENCE AT THE END OF THE REIGN

In Jean Paul Sartre's play, *No Exit*, one of the characters exclaimed, "I died too soon!" but another replies that everyone either dies too soon – or too late. In the case of Elizabeth I, perhaps it was the latter. Wallace Mac-Caffrey describes the two decades that ranged from the mid-1560s to the mid-1580s as the golden years of Elizabeth's reign, with peace and prosperity and a highly popular Queen. MacCaffrey believes that Elizabeth had earned this love and respect of her people through her commitment to the policies of peace abroad and sound economy at home: in her view, the sovereign as active political manager. "Had she died then," MacCaffrey argues, "Elizabeth would have retained among her contemporaries the image of Astraea, the golden age goddess of peace and plenty."[1] The events of the 1580s and 1590s drove Elizabeth into a policy that went against her instincts and England into a period of war that had grave repercussions, and made the English people far more critical of their monarch. Many of those who fought for England and their Queen were never paid and in the 1590s suffered a life of poverty. It was also a time when outsiders were more recognized and more persecuted. The 1590s was the harshest decade in the reign in terms of witchcraft trials, and the targets of the trial were often poorer women. The charge that Dr Roderigo Lopez, an Anglicized Iberian Jew, planned to poison Elizabeth in 1594 gave voice to strong anti-Jewish sentiments, and though the few Africans in England had been brought there against their will, English anxiety over them caused Elizabeth to attempt to expel them in 1601, on the excuse that they were taking jobs away from the English who needed them.

Yet despite all the pain and difficulties of the final years of the reign, it was also a time of great cultural development, and the height of it – the drama of Shakespeare and his contemporaries – was available not only to the Queen and the aristocrats at Court, but to the commoners in London who paid a pittance to stand in the pit at The Globe and watch the plays, or who watched the plays throughout the country when the companies went on tour. The last decade of Elizabeth's reign saw a great burst of cultural activity and achievement as well as hard times for many of its people. There were immense possibilities for ambitious, literate people in England at the end of the sixteenth century. Shakespeare is the most famous, but he was one of a number who saw playwriting as a means to success, though his unique genius transformed the theatrical experience for his age and our own. Scholars have long debated the end of Elizabeth's reign: was it a time of optimism as some of these plays with their patriotic themes and successful characters demonstrate, or a time of great pessimism and anger at the aging Queen for the harsh conditions? But surely there are a multiplicity of experiences and attitudes in any time period, and as the sixteenth century and the long reign of the Queen was drawing to a close, we can find examples of not only hope and pride but also anguish. Moreover, the drama of the 1590s signified a greater blend of cultural experiences than ever before. Playing companies had large theaters especially built for them in the London suburbs, where they were able to put on plays before thousands of people at a time; they offered the same plays at court with the Queen herself as part of, indeed the center of, the audience; in a sense, her response to the play was another level of theatrical experience for the rest of the audience.[2]

This chapter examines both the difficulties at the end of Elizabeth's reign, especially for those on the margins of the society and how such groups – the poor, especially soldiers, witches and other women stepping outside of appropriate behavior, Jews, and Africans were brought into the national dialogue through their representation on the English stage. The harsh problems at the end of the reign – the horrors of war and the ill-treatment of the soldiers, as well as the fear of witches, Jews, Africans, and other foreigners, were transformed by Shakespeare and other playwrights into plays of great power and eloquence as well as popularity in the final decade of Elizabeth's reign and the early years of her successor James I. Shakespeare's representations of Moors, Jews, and witches expressed his ambivalence about "the other"; villains who also had touching moments of humanity;[3] his audience's response was often much more overtly negative, demonstrating the difficulties and fault lines at the end of the sixteenth century.

The wars at the end of the reign cost England a great deal. The financial burden was obvious.[4] Elizabeth began the struggle with Spain with almost £300 000 "chested treasure" in the Exchequer, which came from the savings from an economical government and the wealth brought in by Francis Drake. In 1583 the Exchequer spent £149 000. Five years later, the year of the Armada, the expenditure was £420 000 and in 1599, because of Ireland, over £570 000. By 1599 the Exchequer was empty and the government debt was £177 000. The Crown debt was a highly problematic legacy to James, though his extravagance increased it sharply in the first five years of his reign. To pay for the wars Elizabeth sold off Crown lands, but this short-term solution cut down on her capital. Elizabeth and her government had to rely more and more on her subjects to finance the war. This meant not only a steep increase in Parliamentary taxation, but an even steeper increase in the other ways the Crown raised money, such as the sale of monopolies, which many people deeply resented, especially so those who were represented in Parliament.[5] But monopolies were not the only problematic method used to raise money. Church property was also exploited. For example, the bishopric of Ely had no bishop between 1581 and 1599; during that time the Crown kept absolute control of the revenues there.[6] It was, however, monopolies that caused the crisis with Elizabeth's last Parliament in 1601.

The recipient of the monopoly was licensed to export prohibited goods or was exempted from statutes that regulated the manufacture of important commodities. For most of the reign this was not a problem, but in the 1580s and 1590s Elizabeth exploited the practice as a means to raise money and to keep her courtiers satisfied. The Earl of Essex's ten-year monopoly allowing him to license the sale of sweet wine had brought him a fortune; Elizabeth's refusal to renew it had led to his rebellion. Monopolies were not granted to regulate trade or encourage foreign skills in England, but as a means of patronage to a courtier, or to raise money for the Crown. The recipient exploited the patent by charging higher prices, and this occurred at a time of high inflation. Members of Parliament brought up the abuses of monopolies in the House of Commons in 1597 and Elizabeth promised she would end the abuses. Nothing was done to reform the situation, however, and indeed in the next four years the abuses and grievances became much more intense. Finally, in January 1601 the Council instructed the Solicitor-General,

Thomas Fleming, to proceed against harmful patents, but he did not pursue any action. When Parliament met again in October 1601, members of the House of Commons were furious not only over the abuses, but also over Elizabeth's Privy Council's failure to do anything about these destructive practices.

Many, many goods were on the list of patents, such as currants, iron, steel, glass, vinegar, sea coal, lead, salt. While some of these were luxuries, others were critical necessities. So many new products were becoming monopolies that people sarcastically suggested bread would be the next item. Angry members discussed legislating monopolies, which would have been an attempt to limit or modify the Queen's prerogative right. Some argued that the Crown's granting of exclusive manufacturing and trading rights to a privileged few deprived free men of their livelihoods, a right that had been assured centuries earlier by the Magna Carta.[7] Monopolies caused prices to go up and often, as a result, the production and sale of poorer quality goods, but the most telling argument against them in Parliament was their threat to the vocations of working men. Danger to the welfare of the individual meant danger to the entire commonwealth.

Elizabeth, at the last moment, took control of the situation. She informed the House of Commons that she was appalled to learn of the terrible harm done to her loving subjects by monopolies and that she herself would protect them. She promised to cancel those that caused the most harm, such as those for salt, starch, vinegar, and some other commodities, while suspending others, and any could be challenged in the common law courts. In three days a royal proclamation cancelled the worst of the monopolies and promised punishment to those who had abused the system. The proclamation also, however, asserted the Queen's right to issue patents if she so desired.

But while Elizabeth could tell her subjects that she loved them, at the end of her reign there were not only terrible financial problems for the Crown, but also more poverty in the country than before. One of the ways Elizabeth's government dealt with such problems at the end of the reign was the passage of the Poor Laws, far more comprehensive than the ones passed earlier in the century.[8] The legislation of 1598 and 1601 occurred at a time when the problems caused by poverty were especially severe. As John Guy points out, this legislation improved and extended the previous legislation as well as streamlining its implementation.[9] The harvests of 1596 and 1597 yielded little.[10] Prices were high, while food supplies were scarce. There are a variety of theories as to why the Poor Laws were passed. Some historians argue that, with the rise in population throughout the sixteenth century, there were also more poor people and we should see the Poor Laws as being stimulated by economic circumstances. Others have argued that, because of humanism and Protestantism at the end of the sixteenth century, people had new ideas about what the government ought to do for the poor. Still others argue that the government itself wished to have more control over its subjects. Paul Slack suggests that all of these approaches need to be considered.[11]

The Poor Laws of the end of the sixteenth century sought to distinguish between those who could work but chose instead to be idle and either beg or steal and those who were truly deserving of help. Elizabeth's government wanted to end begging and to have each parish collect poor rates and then distribute them to those truly in need. The legislation at the end of Elizabeth's reign called for the punishment of vagrants, while the disabled poor would receive help that was financed by the compulsory poor rates. Those who refused to pay would be arrested. Employment would be found for those who could work, though all too often no work could be found. The legislation was important in much more clearly defining the roles of those who would oversee help for the poor. A related Act for the Relief of Soldiers and Mariners granted pensions to those who had been wounded in defense of their country. Parliament also passed acts in 1598 and 1601 that called for the building of hospitals and houses of correction, and for the providing of some medical care for the honest poor. The Poor Laws were probably inadequate, and did not alleviate all problems, but they accomplished at least some of their goals and they were the beginning of a realistic national code and an early model of the modern welfare state.

Coinciding with the poverty and the passage of the Poor Laws, the 1590s was also a time of the reign with the highest incidence of witchcraft accusations, and a number of those accused of witchcraft were poorer women. The first statute against witchcraft in England had been passed in 1542 in the reign of Henry VIII, and repealed in 1547 at the beginning of the reign of his son; the 1563 Act Against Conjurations, Inchantments, and Witch Craft was more severe than the earlier one. It was repealed in 1604 and under James I the most severe statute yet was passed, not to be repealed until 1736. There were a variety of ways that someone, almost always a woman, could be found to be a witch, and the evidence accepted was such that few accused could easily escape. We should note, however, that the number of accusations and executions were fewer in England than in Scotland or the Continent, and witchcraft prosecutions were only a small percentage of the indictments for crime in the Elizabethan era.[12] In sixteenth-century England there was less concern with the idea of women selling their souls to the devil, and more concern with using magic to harm one's neighbors through occult means. The two sixteenth-century statutes did not mention the diabolic pact. Very common in English witchcraft trials was "mischief following anger." If a poor woman came to someone's door to beg and, when she was sent away hungry, she muttered some curse that might in later days come true, this could be used as evidence of witchcraft. Scholars have suggested that, in some cases, the breakdown of community and the guilt over refusing to help the needy caused people to accuse poor women of witchcraft.[13]

Shakespeare's audience would have easily recognized this kind of evidence in an early interchange the witches had in *Macbeth*, written and performed only a year or so after Elizabeth's death. When one witch asked the other where she had been, the reply was a clear example of mischief following anger:

> A sailor's wife has chestnuts in her lap,
> and mounched, and mounched, and mounched.
> 'Give me', quoth I.
> 'Aroint thee, witch!' the rump-fed ronyon cries.
>
> (I.iii.4–7)

To punish the sailor's wife the witch explains that "her husband's to Allepo gone, master o' th' Tiger" (I.iii.8). The other witches offer her winds to shake up his ship but she plans to go even further in her revenge. She will "drain him dry as hay," and he will "sleep neither night nor day" (I.iii.18, 19). Her magic will make him dwindle and pine away. A woman guilty over refusing to share food could easily believe a storm was caused or that a husband died because of the witch who had been begging and had been refused.

All too often people were convinced about the witch's guilt even before the curse. This was certainly the case in the 1590s in a trial that was known as the Warboys case. Using this case as an example allows us to put a human face on the witchcraft phenomenon. In 1593 an elderly woman, Alice Samuel, her husband, and her daughter were put on trial for witchcraft and all found guilty.[14] The case had started four years earlier when the daughters of Robert Throckmorton, the wealthiest man in the village of Warboys, had begun to have strange fits. The doctors who were called in suspected witchcraft and the afflicted girls named one of their neighbors, Alice Samuel, a poor, older woman of the village. Alice was forced repeatedly to come to their house and eventually to live with them. At first she accused the girls of "wantonnesse" – of making up their symptoms – but, after years of being told she was a witch who caused these problems, in 1592 she confessed to bewitching the children and causing the death of Lady Cromwell, the wife of the landlord, who had paid a sympathy visit to the Throckmortons and had accused Alice of witchcraft.

When Alice returned to her own home after making her confession, her husband and daughter were appalled and at their urging, she recanted her confession. This so outraged Throckmorton that he had not only the mother arrested but her daughter Agnes as well, and the Throckmorton girls then claimed that Agnes was a far worse witch than her mother was. Though both were indicted and jailed, Throckmorton bailed Agnes out and forced her to live in the family home, where she was constantly questioned and harangued. The spirits that the girls said possessed them also told the children to scratch and beat her. At the trial Alice Samuel, her daughter Agnes, and her husband John, who had also been accused, were all found guilty. Alice Samuel pleaded that she was pregnant, since women convicted of capital crimes were not executed until at least after the child was born if they could prove their pregnancy to a board of matrons.[15] Since Alice Samuel was quite elderly and clearly past the age of childbearing, the entire court burst out in laughter and the judge told her to give up that plea, but Alice insisted on being examined by the board of matrons. After their examination they declared that Alice was not with child, unless, perhaps, it was with the devil and that would be another reason that she should be hanged. Another prisoner suggested to the daughter Agnes that she also make this plea, which would have been more believable given her age. Just as Agnes had always maintained her innocence to the charge, neither would she attempt to save her life by this means, stating, "It shall never be said, that I was both a Witch and a whore."[16] Mother, father, and daughter were all hanged. They were among the thousand or so people, mostly women, who were executed for witchcraft in early modern England.[17]

Just as some poorer women were targeted at the end of the sixteenth century, so too was there concern both about Jews and Africans in England. Jews had been in England in the earlier Middle Ages. After 1218 Jews were required to wear distinctive badges so that they would not be confused with Christians, and there was more and more violence against them. In 1290 Edward I formally expelled them on pain of death, and only a very few who converted to Christianity stayed.[18] A small number of them began to return in the early sixteenth century, however, though they were not formally allowed back into England until the 1650s. Despite, or because of, their banishment, by the thirteenth century the term "Jew" had become part of the English vocabulary as a catchall term of abuse, often directed at other Christians. "I hate thee as I do a Jew," was a common saying.[19]

Especially at times of great social/cultural change, one of the ways for a group to self-define is to exclude all who are – or have characteristics of – difference. As we have seen, religious experience was tumultuous for most Elizabethans in later sixteenth-century England. Their grandparents turned from Rome to the Church of England under Henry VIII, while their parents might have reverted to Catholicism under Mary, before changing their faith again with the accession of Elizabeth. As James Shapiro points out, in the decades after the break with Rome in the 1530s and the establishment of the Reformation,

> the English began to think of the Jews not only as a people who almost three centuries earlier had been banished from English territory but also as a potential threat to the increasingly permeable boundaries of their own social and religious identities. The challenge of preserving these boundaries was intensified by the difficulties of pointing to physical characteristics that unmistakably distinguished English Christians from Jews.[20]

From 1290 until the end of the fifteenth century, there is no evidence of organized communities of Jews in England. But by the reign of Henry VIII, there was a secret Jewish community in London with a secret synagogue, financial support, and business connections with Antwerp. In the late 1530s and 1540s it consisted of about 100 people. The records also hint at the importance of Jewish women in cooking ritual meals and helping to maintain the religion in secret. A number of the musicians who played for the King were also Italians of Jewish origin. Henry VIII employed 19 of these musicians at court. This group assimilated quickly and intermarried with the English so that their children and grandchildren were practicing Christians, only partially aware of their Jewish origins. One of these was the early seventeenth-century poet Aemelia Bassano Lanier, daughter of court musician Baptist Bassano.

There were also some secretly observant Jews in Bristol and some connections between the London and the Bristol communities. In the late 1540s and early 1550s the community in Bristol held religious services in the house of Henrique Nuñez, and Yom Kippur was observed as well as the Sabbath and festivals. Nuñez's wife, Beatriz Fernandes, taught new Jewish immigrants prayers and baked the unleavened bread for Passover. Nuñez, as was the case for the other members of the community, while outwardly a member of the Anglican Church, continued to practice his own faith in secret.[21]

In 1580 Portugal became part of Spain, and did not separate from it again until 1640; Philip II continued his anti-Jewish policy throughout the Iberian peninsula. A number of Jewish Portuguese refugees were permitted to come to England as long as they agreed to conform to the state religion. Elizabeth's Council used a number of these Portuguese Jews as sources of intelligence; many of those involved were also in trade.[22] We know of one specific case that was tried in the court of Chancery in 1596, between Mary May, a widow of the merchant Richard May, and two Portuguese Jews, Ferdinand Alvares and Alvaro de Lyma, who for a time were resident in the same street as the Mays. The widow May claimed a debt from them due to her husband's estate because of some ventures in trade that had begun in 1586. The trading venture that they had with her husband had cost a great deal more that she thought it ought because her husband's Portuguese partners and agents were practicing Jews, which she considered a "heinous crime," and they were forced to bribe officials to save their lives and the goods. The evidence from the trial showed that Mary May tried to prove that her London neighbors Alvares and de Lyma "were practicing Jews, and no Christians in truth, whatever their pretenses."[23] Other evidence at the trial suggests that indeed, while there was a community of Jews in London in the 1590s who went to the Anglican Church, in their households they practiced their observances solemnly and in secret. Though the parish records show the marriages and deaths of the members of the Jewish colony, there is no record of any baptism for their children. The May trial ended in a compromise, with Mrs May agreeing to forego some of her claims. Alverez's brother-in-law, Dr Hector Nuñuz, though an active parishioner of the parish of St Olaves' in Hart Street, in his will clearly proclaimed his Jewish identity, however, it was only in ways that would be readily understood by fellow Jews.

But still, if a Jew became too successful, no matter what he did to pass, he could still be targeted and the anti-Jewish attitudes of the English people would come to the foreground. Indeed, some people did not consider even Jews who converted to Christianity "true Christians." Many argued that being a Jew cannot "be washed [away] – with the sacred tincture of baptism" and referred to such as "baptised Jews," or "counterfeit Christians."[24] For many of the late sixteenth/early seventeenth century, a sincere Jewish conversion was a paradox, an impossibility. While some of the English hoped that if Jews were to come to England, they could be converted, others feared their presence would weaken Christian belief, suggesting a strange power Jews would have over Christians. For William Prynne, a Puritan pamphleteer, it was far too risky to allow many Jews into England, since "thousands" of Christians would "in probability turn apostate Jews, instead of converting any of the Jews to Christianity."[25]

The most notorious Jew at the end of the Elizabethan age was the physician Roderigo Lopez, who outwardly practiced the Anglican faith. Lopez, of Portuguese Jewish background and trained as a physician, came to England in 1559. He had studied medicine at Italian universities, was married, and he and his wife Sarah had three daughters and two sons. Sarah was a daughter of the rich Dunstan Anes, a banker who, though outwardly Christian, was one of the leaders of the Jewish community in England. Lopez was so skilled he soon gained the highest renown as a physician. He was the first to be named to the office of house physician at St Bartholomew's Hospital and he also joined the College of Physicians. By the early 1570s he was treating some major figures at Court, such as Sir Francis Walsingham and Robert Dudley, the Earl of Leicester. By 1584 Lopez was famous enough to be targeted. In *Leicester's Commonwealth*, an anonymous scurrilous attack on Dudley, it is "Lopez, the Jew" who is described as being particularly skilled in poisons. Despite such attacks, two years later he was appointed Elizabeth's chief physician.

In the 1590s – at the same time there was such a burst of cultural development with the plays of Marlowe and Shakespeare – the Court was changing as the Queen was getting elderly. Many of the advisors and courtiers on whom she had depended were gone. Her dearest favorite, Leicester, died in 1588 and Sir Francis Walsingham, whose spy system had kept her safe during the long threat of Mary Stuart's imprisonment in England, had died in 1590. Though her closest advisor, William Cecil, Lord Burghley, was still with her, he was getting elderly, and had handed over some of his work to his son Robert. Leicester's stepson, the Earl of Essex, and Robert Cecil were battling for control of the Council and influence over Elizabeth in the early 1590s.

In 1594 Essex was desperate for success in the eyes of both Elizabeth and the London mob. He achieved a spectacular – if, to us today, dubious success.[26] After Walsingham's death, Essex developed his own spy system.

Essex wanted Elizabeth to see how well his intelligence service worked. He did not want her to believe herself to be safe, but wanted her to give him the credit for saving her from danger by exposing the dangerous plots against her. Essex wanted Elizabeth to believe that it was him, and him only, who could provide her with the protection that she needed. As a result, Elizabeth's security became intertwined with the struggle to dominate the Court.

Lopez was an easy target for Essex. Despite his outward practice of Christianity, he was perceived as a Jew, alien, and dangerous. Moreover, Essex may have had a specific grudge against Lopez, whom he felt was not deferential enough. Essex and his supporters started a public campaign against Lopez. They made fun of him. They contemptuously referred to him as "the Jew." He had become, suddenly, very conspicuous, singled out, and targeted. On Essex's insistence Lopez was arrested for planning to poison Elizabeth. For a long time Lopez staunchly maintained his innocence despite remorseless interrogation and the threat of torture, but, when confronted with these claims, he finally broke down. He confessed "that he had indeed spoken of this matter [Elizabeth's murder] and promised it, but all to cozen the King of Spain." He said that Walsingham had asked him to establish contacts with the Spanish court and had used him to pass false information to the enemy. Unfortunately for Lopez, Walsingham was dead and thus could not confirm his story. While a number of scholars today see the case against Lopez as frabricated, David Katz argues that he was indeed guilty.[27] One can still, however, doubt Essex's role and motives in the case whether Lopez was actually guilty or not.

Essex was elated and thought the facts of the case were clear. He wrote to a friend, "I have discovered a most dangerous and desperate treason. The point of conspiracy was her Majesty's death. The executioner should have been Dr Lopez; the manner poison. This I have so followed as I will make it appear as clear as noon day." No time was lost. Within 48 hours of his confession Lopez was on trial for conspiracy to murder Elizabeth. When Lopez came to trial in February 1594, his assertions that his so-called confession was extorted under threat of the rack was ignored. His prosecution was conducted by Sir Edward Coke, the Solicitor-General, who described Lopez as "a perjured and murdering villain and Jewish doctor, worse than Judas himself." Lopez was found guilty and condemned, despite his affirmation that he had "never thought harm to her majesty." Spectators showed their approval with enthusiastic applause. "All the world" approved the verdict, suggested one spectator. Elizabeth herself seems to have had her doubts, and delayed execution for three months before finally bowing to pressure and allowing Lopez's execution that June. His execution was an occasion for the most riotous celebration.[28]

Sarah Lopez begged Elizabeth for help two months after her husband's execution, "In consideration of her afflicted and miserable estate", since she "and her poor children are innocent of her husband's crime." She was "the sorrowful mother of five comfortless and distressed children born in the realm (three of them being maiden children)." She requested the return of the lease of their house, her household and other goods taken from her during her husband's first imprisonment, certain plate, the licenses of sumac and aniseed belonging to Lopez, and "a parsonage of £30 a year given by the Queen to Anthony, one of her miserable children, for his maintenance at school and learning." Anthony was studying at Winchester. Elizabeth was sympathetic to this request. She restored the lease at Mountjoy's Inn which he held from Winchester College and also the goods and chattels not exceeding £100 forfeit by the attainder.[29]

The public Jew-baiting and hysteria from the Lopez case led to a revival of Christopher Marlowe's earlier play, *The Jew of Malta*, which was composed about 1589–90, and was frequently performed in the last decade of the sixteenth century and the first decade of the seventeenth century. Between 1592 and 1596 it was put on at least 36 times. During the week of Lopez's execution Philip Henslowe noted in his diary six performances of the play. Its renewed popularity probably led to the composition of Shakespeare's *Merchant of Venice*.[30]

In *The Merchant of Venice*, the Jewish moneylender Shylock demands a pound of flesh from the merchant Antonio when Antonio cannot repay his debt. It is only the heroine Portia's cleverness, while disguised as a lawyer, that saves Antonio. The character Shylock, possibly played by the actor Richard Burbage in the 1590s, may have appeared on stage with a red beard, which would have been a popularly recognized sign of Judas, and a fake nose; he would have been roundly booed by the audience. Yet Shakespeare also gives Shylock the speech that argues for the Jews' humanity:

Hath not a Jew eyes? Hath not a Jew hands, organs, dimensions, senses, affections, passions? – fed with the same food, hurt with the same weapons, subject to the same diseases, healed by the same means, warmed and cooled by the same winter and summer as a Christian is?

If you prick us, do we not bleed? If you tickle us, do we not laugh? If you poison us, do we not die? And if you wrong us, shall we not revenge? If we are like you in the rest, we will resemble you in that.

(III.i.46–53)

While Elizabethan audiences may have ignored or belittled that speech, in modern productions it is often the centerpiece of the play, the reminder that there was diversity in Elizabethan England as well, and that those who were different deserved respect.

Just as Jews were presented on the English stage, so too were Africans. In Shakespeare's early play *Titus Andronicus*, the villain Aaron was a Moor who is definitely presented as a black man, though the term "Moor" had a multiplicity of meanings in that time. "Let fools do good, and fair men call for grace, Aaron will have his soul black like his face" (III.i.204–5). While the Moor was nameless and merely a tool of the wicked Queen Tamora in the late-medieval prose history that was Shakespeare's source, Aaron is a far more developed character.[31] The other characters label him with almost every term that Europeans used to denigrate Africans: "incarnate devil," "coal-black Moor," "wall-eyed slave," "black dog," "barbarous Moor," "accursed devil," and "inhuman dog," the latter two also used against Shylock in *Merchant*. And Aaron, in his multiple villainies, confirms the expectations of an Elizabethan audience who viewed Moors as more diabolical than human.[32] But in spite of his villainy, Aaron is also given human feelings and pride in his blackness:

> Is black so base a hue?
>   . . .
> Coal-black is better than another hue,
> In that it scorns to bear another hue.
> (IV.ii.71, 100–1)

While the nurse describes Tamora's baby, whom Aaron had fathered, as "joyless, dismal, black . . . loathsome as a toad," (IV.ii. 67–8), Aaron does all he can to protect his son. Eldred Jones argues that at the end of the play, Shakespeare moves away from Aaron as monster to a loving, protective parent. By the time Shakespeare composed *Othello*, his title character was a much more textured character, even though he ended up a murderer.

Shakespeare's plays were not, however, the only representations of Africans in Elizabethan England. In the sixteenth century a number of books were published that typify the sources of popular ideas about Africa.[33] They solidified views of Africa as being filled with monstrous races that had been increasingly common since the thirteenth century.[34] William Waterman's *The Fardle of Facions conteining the auncient maners, customes and lawes of the peoples enhabiting the two parts of the earth called Affrike and Asie* thoroughly relied on the ancient authorities' bizarre tales and descriptions, and made the old legends readily available for English readers. Waterman described the people of "Ethiope" as monstrous in shape. His descriptions of monstrosity and wild sexual behavior would have fascinated his readers, as well as making the Africans seem utterly alien. "It is the manner among [The Nasamones], for every man to have many wives: and the fellowship of their wives, that others use in secret: they use in open sight." Another group is similar in its promiscuity and lack of what the English would consider moral values. The Ichthiophagi were described as going naked for their entire lives, and sharing their wives and children in common. Waterman added that they ate shellfish together in the wild field with great merriment, and after they ate, they would "fall upon their women, even as they come to hand without any choice."[35] Eldred Jones argues that the statements in such a book as Waterman's "would have cemented in the popular mind notions of dark-skinned people as carefree and lustful, notions that were taken for granted by mid-century."[36]

Richard Eden's translation of Peter Martyr's *Decades of the New World*, published in 1555, included two published accounts of actual voyages Englishmen made to Africa in the sixteenth century. Even in Eden's book, eyewitness accounts are mixed in with material from classical authors. The process of replacing myths with new information had begun, though it was a slow transformation. Eden published, along with his translation of Peter Martyr, the accounts of Thomas Windham's voyage to Guinea in 1553. What is perhaps most interesting is how Eden's negative generalizations about Africa contradict the firsthand accounts he himself includes. In the introduction Eden describes the people of all the regions of Guinea as idolaters and savages who do not profess any religion, or other knowledge of God, than by the law of nature.[37] Yet in the account of Windham's visit to Benin, a very different picture emerges. "When they came they were brought with a great company to the presence of the king [of Benin], who being a black Moor (although not so black as the rest) sat in a great huge hall, long and wide...And here to speak of the great reverence they give to their king, being such that if we would give as much to our Savior Christ, we should remove from our heads many plagues which we daily deserve for our contempt and impiety."[38] The King was also fluent in Portuguese, which he had learned as a child, and thus was able to speak with the travelers. Jones points out the contradiction: "Somehow this account of an actual meeting with a civilized, bilingual, black king in Guinea (he had even offered the strangers credit until their next voyage) did not impress Eden enough to make him modify the sweeping generalizations he had 'gathered' for his preface."[39]

It seems, then, that the image of Africa that emerges from the knowledge held by the sixteenth-century English is a blend of a number of sources. But people of England of the sixteenth century also saw actual Africans, as well as reading about them in travel books and seeing their depictions on the stage. Elizabethans knew Africans as free people, but they also knew them as slaves. They traded with them, they captured them, and sometimes they killed them. Africans were at the same time known and yet mysterious. And the people of Tudor England were intensely suspicious of all foreigners, perceiving them as curious and inferior. They were highly critical of the French, the Spanish, and the Italians. They conceived of the Irish as savages. It is hardly surprising they held such negative views of Africans, especially when many of the "Moors," as they called them, were also not Christians. A common sixteenth-century proverb stated that three Moors were equal to one Portuguese, and three Portuguese equal to one Englishman.[40]

Yet the word "Moor" had no clear racial status in sixteenth-century terms. Elizabethan authors describe "Moors" as existing all over the globe, but only in that outer circle of the non-Christian savage world.[41] For example, there are descriptions of "Moors" in Asia. Some "Moors" are described as black and others as "tawny." But though some of these sixteenth-century authors might be vague about their geography, they were certainly precise in their sense of an antithetical relationship between "Moors" (wherever they lived) and civilized white Christians.[42]

The sixteenth-century English also held the deeply rooted and ancient belief that black is the color of sin and death, a strongly held cultural tradition. Black was used to mean "having sinister or deadly purposes," or something "atrocious and horribly wicked." In 1583 Philip Stubbes wrote in *Anatomy of Abuses* of "many a black curse" and William Lambarde warned followers of Mary Queen of Scots in 1581, "You will have a black soul... if you do not the sooner forsake the Queen." Black could also mean "clouded with sorrow or melancholy; dismal, gloomy, sad." Part of the Christian mythology of the Middle Ages and early modern period was to see devils and demons as black men. Two fifteenth-century English mystics, Margery Kempe and Julian of Norwich, described devils as monstrous black men.[43] Even though Reginald Scot debunked many superstitions in *The Discovery of Witchcraft* [1584], he did state that "a damned soul may and does take the shape of a black moor." In the 1581 trial of Cicely Celles, a demonic imp appeared to a little boy, looking just like his sister, "but that it was all black."[44]

The view of devils as black men certainly influenced how actual Africans were viewed and treated. Thomas Windham brought two "Moors," described as "noble men" back to England from his first voyage to North Africa in 1551, and subsequently returned them to their home, according to James Alday, a servant to Sebastian Cabot.[45] In 1555 John Lok brought a group of five black Africans to England that he described as "certain black slaves, whereof some were tall and strong men, and could well agree with our meats and drinks. The cold and moist air does somewhat offend them." This did not seem to bother Lok as he continued, "Yet doubtless men that are born in hot Regions may better abide cold, than men that are born in cold Regions may abide hot."[46] Three were known as Binne, Anthonie, and George. We do not have names, real or adopted, of the other two. They came from the town of Shama, on the coast of what is now Ghana. The English believed that they needed African help if they were to break the Portuguese hold on trade there, so Lok, son of a prominent London merchant and alderman, brought the group of West Africans to England. The idea was that they should learn English and then go back to Africa as interpreters and "friends" of the English. Another London merchant, William Towerson, returned three of the Africans to their home on a subsequent voyage in 1556, and they were soon helping Towerson by convincing other Africans that it was safe to board his ships for trading purposes. They acted as interpreters and public relations men for him in West Africa. When on one occasion the inhabitants in one area refused to trade with Towerson, he used one of the Africans with him to smooth the way: "We found a fair bay where we ran in and found a small town . . . but the Negroes for a long time would not come to us, but at the last by the persuasion of our own Negroes, one boat came to us, and with him we sent George our Negro ashore, and after he had talked with them, they came aboard our boats without fear." When the returning travelers finally got back to their home, they were enthusiastically welcomed. At Hanta, not far from their home town of Shama, an eyewitness stated, "our Negroes were well known, and the men of the town wept for joy, when they saw them, and demanded of them where Anthonie and Binne had been: and they told them that they had been at London in England, and should be brought home the next voyage." At Shama itself, their relatives rushed out to greet them with great joy, as did the others in the town. This sense of affection and family feeling surprised the English observers, who did not expect "savages" to have such emotions.[47]

The English involvement with Africans was, however, to become even more pernicious. The myths about the Africans allowed the English to have easy consciences about their participation in the slave trade.[48] In the 1560s sea dogs such as John Hawkins started their active participation in the slave trade; the English became even more involved in the late seventeenth century.[49] As a by-product of this beginning involvement, African slaves were brought to England from the 1570s onward in small numbers. In the late sixteenth century they were used in England in three capacities: as household servants (most of them had this status), as prostitutes for wealthy English and Dutch men, and as court entertainers.

Records of the time provide a number of examples. In 1570 Nicholas Wichehalse of Barnstaple in Devon mentioned "Anthony my negro" in his will. The illegitimate daughter of Mary, who was described as "a negro of John Whites" was baptized in Plymouth in 1594. The father was a Dutch man. In 1598 there was an assessment of "Strangers" in Barking (All Hallows parish, Tower ward) which mentioned several "Negroes," all of whom were servants. Sir Walter Raleigh and his wife had a black servant or slave, as did the Earl of Dorset. There were also some black entertainers at court. In the late 1570s a beautiful coat was made for a young black entertainer and there are records of several other black musicians and boy dancers at Elizabeth's court.[50]

By the end of the century, in fact, Queen Elizabeth had begun to be "discontented" at the "great numbers of Negars and Blackamoors which . . . are crept into this realm," and issued two edicts, one in 1599 and a stronger one in 1601, in which she complained of the influx and appointed a certain Caspar van Zenden (Zeuden), a merchant of Lubeck, to transport them out of the country. The 1601 decrees reads:

> After our hearty commendations; whereas the Queen's Majesty, tendering the good and welfare of her own natural subjects greatly distressed in these hard times of dearth, is highly discontented to understand the great numbers of . . . Blackamoors which (as she is informed) are crept into this realm . . . who are fostered and relieved

here to the great annoyance of her own liege people that want the relief which those people consume; as also for that the most of them are infidels, having no understanding of Christ or his Gospel, hath given especial commandment that the said kind of people should be with all speed . . . discharged out of this Her Majesty's dominions. And to that end and purpose hath appointed Caspar van Zenden, merchant of Lubeck for their speedy transportation . . . And if there shall be any person or persons which are possessed of any such Blackamoors that refuse to deliver them in sort as aforesaid, then we require you to call them before you and to advise and persuade them by all good means to satisfy Her Majesty's pleasure therein, which if they shall eftsoons willfully and obstinately refuse, we pray you then to certify their names unto us, to the end Her Majesty may take such further course therein as it shall seem best in her princely wisdom.[51]

Even though the proclamation described most of the blacks in England as "infidels having no understanding of Christ or his gospel," as Emeka Abanime remarks, "the solicitude shown for Christianity in the Queen's proclamation is not very convincing. In the first place, at least some of the blacks in the kingdom were already Christians . . . [but] the expulsion order made no exception in favour of christianized blacks."[52] It should be no surprise that these edicts of Elizabeth's happened at the same times as the Poor Laws. But while the end of the 1590s was a time of inflation, bad harvests, and destitution for many of the English, expelling the few blacks who were in England at the time would hardly solve these serious problems. Despite this order, some blacks stayed in England, and in the seventeenth century more were brought in.

England at the end of Elizabeth's reign experienced a time of great cultural achievement, but for those on the margins, some of the poor, older women, Jews, or Africans, it could also be treacherous. And the representations of these figures on the public stage brought them into cultural consciousness more than ever before. Though problems with foreign and domestic policy, relations between Church and State, were not solved in Elizabeth's reign and by the reign of her next successor but one, England was to be engulfed in a civil war between monarch and Parliament, the England of the second half of the sixteenth century was also a time of remarkable accomplishment. MacCaffrey is probably correct that Elizabeth's reputation would have been greater had her reign ended 15 years earlier, yet the entire reign was a remarkable time, with great accomplishments as well as serious problems, and the achievements of the reign, as well as the failings, are inextricably connected with the ruler.

In 1601, as was noted earlier in the chapter, the House of Commons had been elated when Elizabeth finally agreed to deal with the problems of the monopolies and they wished to thank the Queen. The Speaker and the 140 members of the House of Commons he brought with him assembled on 30 November so that they could thank their Queen. Elizabeth's response to them is known as her Golden Speech, and was the final speech of her reign before Parliament. In it she talked about her duty as a monarch, her great love for her people, and how much she valued the love they had for her.

> Though God hath raised Me high; yet This I count the Glory of my Crown, That I have Reigned with your Loves...I do not so much rejoice, That God hath made Me to be a Queen, as To be a Queen over so Thankful a People.... There will never Queen sit in my Seat with more Zeal to my Country, Care for my Subjects, and that sooner with willingness will venture her Life for your Good and Safety, than My Self. For it is not my desire to Live nor Reign longer, than my Life and Reign shall be for your Good. And though you have had, and may have many Princes, more Mighty and Wise, sitting this State; yet you never had, or shall have any that will be more Careful and Loving.[53]

The rhetoric, alas, was often more effective than the reality. But Elizabeth's amazing personality not only shaped her own century so it is known as the Elizabethan Age, but hundreds of years later her image still fascinates us. At the end of the twentieth century, people still flocked to the movie theaters to see a film simply titled, *Elizabeth*.

NOTES

Introduction

1. "By the end of Elizabeth's reign the number of aliens in London had swelled to upwards of ten thousand, in a population that has been estimated at somewhere between one hundred and fifty and two hundred thousand." James Shapiro, *Shakespeare and the Jews* (New York: Columbia University Press), 75.
2. Very useful on the historiographical views of Elizabeth are C. H. Williams, "In Search of the Queen," in *Elizabethan Government and Society: Essays Presented to Sir John Neale*, ed. S. T. Bindoff, Joel Hurstfield, and C. H. Willliams (London: The Athlone Press, 1961), 1–20; Richard L. Greaves, ed., *Elizabeth I, Queen of England* (Lexington, MA: D. C. Heath and Co., 1974); Joseph Levine, ed., *Elizabeth I* (Englewood Cliffs, NJ: Prentice-Hall, Inc., 1969).
3. William Allen, *A True, Sincere, and Modest Defense of English Catholics*, ed. Robert M. Kingdon (Ithaca, NY: Cornell University Press, 1965). Nicholas Sander, *The Rise and Growth of the Anglican Schism. pub A. D. 1585, with a continuation of the History, by the Rev. Edward Rishton*, trans. and ed. David Lewis (London: Burns and Oates, 1877).
4. John Lingard, *The History of England from the First Invasion by the Romans to the Accession of William and Mary in 1688*, 6th edn (London: C. Dolman, 1854); James Froude, *The History of England from the Fall of Wolsey to the Defeat of the Spanish Armada* (New York: C. Scribner and Co., 1870–73).
5. John Neale, *Queen Elizabeth I* (1934; rpt. Garden City, NY: Anchor Books, 1957); *Queen Elizabeth and Her Parliaments, 1559–1581* (London: Jonathan Cape, 1953); *Queen Elizabeth and Her Parliaments, 1584–1601* (London: Jonathan Cape, 1957).
6. For example, see Wallace T. MacCaffrey, *Elizabeth I: War and Politics, 1588–1603* (Princeton, NJ: Princeton University Press, 1992) and *Elizabeth I* (London and New York: E. Arnold, 1993); Susan Doran, *Elizabeth I and Religion, 1558–1603* (London and New York: Routledge, 1994) and *Monarchy & Matrimony: The Courtships of Elizabeth I* (London and New York: Routledge, 1996); Anne Somerset, *Elizabeth I* (New York: St. Martin's Press – now Palgrave, 1992); Susan Frye, *Elizabeth I: The Competition for Representation* (New York: Oxford University Press, 1993); Helen Hackett, *Virgin Mother, Maiden Queen: Elizabeth I and the Cult of the Virgin Mary* (London: Macmillan – now Palgrave, 1995); Susan Bassnett, *Elizabeth I: A Feminist Perspective* (Oxford: Berg, 1988); Christopher Haigh, *Elizabeth I* (London and New York: Longman, 1988); Rosalind Kay Marshall, *Elizabeth I* (London: HMSO, 1991); Geffrey Regan, *Elizabeth I: Documents and Commentary* (Cambridge:

Cambridge University Press, 1988); Jasper Ridley, *Elizabeth* (London: Constable, 1987). *Elizabeth I: Collected Works*, ed. Leah S. Marcus, Janel Mueller, and Mary Beth Rose (Chicago, IL: the University of Chicago Press, 2000). Interpretations by the various historians who have written about Elizabeth will be addressed throughout the book.

1 Overview of Elizabeth's Life and Reign

1. As Retha Warnicke points out. "Family and kinship relations at the Henrician court," in *Tudor Political Culture*, ed. Dale Hoak (Cambridge: Cambridge University Press, 1995), 31. [essay runs from 31–53]
2. Elizabeth and her parliaments will be discussed throughout the text. For more specific sources on this issue, the classic work is Neale, *Queen Elizabeth and Her Parliaments, 1559–1581* and *Queen Elizabeth and Her Parliaments, 1584–1601*. For modifications and critiques, see T. E. Hartley, *Elizabeth's Parliaments: Queen, Lords, and Commons, 1559–1601* (Manchester: Manchester University Press,, 1992); D. M. Dean and N. L. Jones, eds, *The Parliaments of Elizabethan England* (Oxford: Basil Blackwell, 1990); D. M. Dean, *Law-Making and Society in Elizabethan England: The Parliament of England, 1584–1601* (Cambridge and New York: Cambridge University Press, 1996); G. R. Elton, *The Parliament of England, 1559–1581* (Cambridge: Cambridge University Press, 1986); Michael A. R. Graves, *Elizabethan Parliaments, 1559–1601* (London, New York: Longman, 1987).
3. David Starkey, *Elizabeth: Apprenticeship* (London: Chatto and Windus, 2000), 42.
4. James McConica and John N. King argue that Katherine's concern for learning and religion were important lessons for Elizabeth, and had a great impact on her development both at the time and later when she was Queen. Maria Dowling, however, counters that Parr's own ability, and thus her impact on Elizabeth, have been overstated. King, "Patronage and Piety: The Influence of Catherine Parr," in Margaret P. Hannay, ed., *Silent But for the Word: Tudor Women as Patrons, Translators, and Writers of Religious Works* (Kent, OH: Kent State University Press, 1985), 43–60; James McConica, *English Humanists and Reformation Politics under Henry VIII and Edward VI* (Oxford: Clarendon Press, 1965), 7, 215–17; Maria Dowling, *Humanism in the Age of Henry VIII* (London: Croom Helm, 1986), 235.
5. Neale, *Elizabeth and her Parliaments*, I, 149; Somerset, *Elizabeth*, 11;
6. As Starkey points out. *Elizabeth: Apprenticeship*.
7. MacCaffrey, *Elizabeth I*, 11; John Foxe, *Acts and Monuments*, ed. Stephen Reed Cattley (London: R. B. Seeley and W. Burnside, 1838), VIII, 603.
8. Letter to Johann Sturm, April 4, 1550, *Letters of Roger Ascham*, trans. Maurice Hatch and Alvin Vos, ed. Alvin Vos (New York: Peter Lang, 1989), 165.
9. Dale Hoak believes the "scheme to alter the succession originated in Northumberland's camp and not in King Edward's brain," "Rehabilitating the Duke of Northumberland," in *The Mid-Tudor Polity, c. 1540–1560*, ed. Robert Tittler and Jennifer Loach (Totowa, NJ: Rowman and Littlefield, 1980), 48. D. M. Loades, however, convincingly argues that W. K. Jordan was right, that the idea to subvert the succession was Edward's, and "that the king's obsessive determination presented [Northum-

berland] with a gambler's opportunity." *John Dudley, Duke of Northumberland, 1504–1553* (Oxford and New York: Oxford University Press, 1996), 241. Diarmaid MacCulloch calls Northumberland's failure "one of the greatest surprises of sixteenth-century English politics." He attributes Mary's success to the wide appeal of legitimism and the careful avoidance of religious issues as Mary fought for her rights. *The Later Reformation in England, 1547–1603* (New York: St. Martin's Press – now Palgrave, 1990), 19, 20.

10. MacCaffrey, *Elizabeth I*, 18.

11. Foxe, *Acts and Monuments*, VIII, 609.

12. John Guy, "Tudor Monarch and Political Culture," in John Morrill, ed., *The Oxford Illustrated History of Tudor & Stuart Britain* (Oxford and New York: Oxford University Press, 1996), 234. According to Gerry Bowler, the anonymous tract, *Certain Questions Demanded and asked by the Noble Realm of England, of her True Natural Children and Subjects of the Same*, published in Wesel spring 1555, was the first of the exile works to claim that no woman could legitimately rule. "Marian Protestants and the Idea of violent Resistance," in Peter Lake and Maria Dowling, eds, *Protestantism and the National Church in Sixteenth-Century England* (London: Croom Helm, 1987), 128. For the early part of the reign, see Wallace MacCaffrey, *The Shaping of the Elizabethan Regime* (Princeton, NJ: Princeton University Press, 1968); Norman Jones, *The Birth of the Elizabethan Age: England in the 1560s* (Oxford: Blackwell, 1993).

13. Loades, *John Dudley*, 284.

14. John Guy, "The 1590s? The Second Reign of Elizabeth I," in John Guy, ed., *The Reign of Elizabeth I: Court and Culture in the Last Decade* (Cambridge: Cambridge University Press, published in association with the Folger Institute, Washington DC, 1995), 13.

15. As pointed out by R. B. Wernham, *The Making of Elizabethan Foreign Policy, 1558–1603* (Berkeley: University of California Press, 1980), 10.

16. For more on the development of the Privy Council, see Penry Williams, *The Later Tudors: England, 1547–1603* (Oxford: Clarendon Press, 1995), 131–5.

17. Haigh, *Elizabeth I*, 36. It is important to note, however, as John Guy points out, the numbers of the working Privy Councillors who regularly attended meetings was about 19 in Mary's reign. Mary had appointed a number of men as a means of reward for loyalty, but they did not often attend. Guy, "Tudor Monarch and Political Culture," 231.

18. Cited in Williams, *The Later Tudors*, 135.

19. Williams, *The Later Tudors*, 137.

20. MacCaffrey, *Queen Elizabeth and the making of Policy, 1572–1588* (Princeton, NJ: Princeton University Press, 1981), 343; Haigh, *Elizabeth I*, 123.

21. Haigh suggests that the pressure on Elizabeth to marry came not from the belief that the men around Elizabeth thought that women were incapable, but from the need for an heir, suggesting if that were the case, they would want to rule for her themselves, not get a king. "They sought not a consort for the Queen but a father for her son – not a sovereign, but a stud." *Elizabeth I*, 10–11. But they did try at the beginning to rule for her, and the rhetoric they used about Elizabeth marrying and having a child was very different from that used toward a male sovereign. For a more thorough discussion of the difference in rhetoric, see Carole Levin, "'We shall never have a merry world while the Queene lyveth':

Gender, Monarchy, and the Power of Seditious Words," in Julia Walker, ed., *Dissing Elizabeth: Negative Representations of Gloriana* (Durham, NC: Duke University Press, 1998), 77–95. As Lacey Baldwin Smith points out, there was a degree of anger and desperation in the comments made. *Elizabeth Tudor: Portrait of a Queen* (Boston, MA: Little, Brown, 1975), 120–2.

22. Jones, *The Birth of the Elizabethan Age*, 132.
23. On 8 September 1560, she was found dead with her neck broken at the bottom of some stairs in the country house where she was living. Though there was a strong popular belief that Robert had had her killed, it seems more likely that she either committed suicide or, indeed, may have simply died accidentally, her spine so brittle from metastasized cancer from which she was suffering that even the act of walking down stairs – especially if she stumbled could have caused her neck to snap. See Ian Aird, "The Death of Amy Robsart: Accident, Suicide, or Murder – or Disease?" *English Historical Review*, 71, 278 (1956), 69–79.
24. On this issue, see particularly the work of Simon Adams, "Factions and Favourites at the Elizabethan Court," in R. G. Asch and A. M. Birke, eds, *Princes, Patronage and Nobility: The Court at the Beginning of the Modern Age, c.1450–1650* (Oxford and New York: Oxford University Press, 1991), 265–87, "Faction, Clientage and Party: English Politics, 1550–1603," *History Today*, 32 (December, 1982), 33–9, "Eliza Enthroned? The Court and its Politics" in Christopher Haigh, *The Reign of Elizabeth I* (Athens: University of Georgia Press, 1985), 55–77. See also, Adams, "The patronage of the crown in Elizabethan politics: the 1590s in perspective," Natalie Mears, "Regnum Cecilianum? A Cecillian perspective of the Court," and Paul E. J. Hammer, "Patronage at Court, faction and the earl of Essex," in Guy, ed., *The Reign of Elizabeth I: Court and Culture in the Last Decade*, 20–45, 46–64, 65–86.

2   Religious Divides and the Religious Settlement

1. Excellent short surveys on this issue are Doran, *Elizabeth I and Religion*; MacCulloch, *The Later Reformation in England*; and David Loades, *Revolution in Religion: The English Reformation, 1530–1570* (Cardiff: University of Wales Press, 1992).
2. Jones, *The Birth of the Elizabethan Age: England in the 1560s*, 19.
3. The leading proponents of this perspective are Christopher Haigh, *English Reformations: Religion, Politics, and Society under the Tudors* (Oxford: Clarendon Press, 1993); and J. J. Scarisbrick, *The Reformation and the English People* (Oxford: Blackwell, 1984). They are responding to and criticizing the arguments especially of A. G. Dickens, *The English Reformation* (2nd edn, University Park: Pennsylvania State University Press, 1991), who argues for a long tradition of Lollard and anti-Catholic popular thought. For a good discussion of the various schools of thought, see Loades, *Revolution in Religion*, 1–5, and especially his comments on page 4; and G. W. Bernard, "The Church of England, *c.*1529–*c.*1642," *History*, 75 (1990), 183–206. See also, Diarmaid MacCulloch, "The Myth of the English Reformation," *Journal of British Studies*, 30 (1991), 1–19.

Notes

127

4. For a discussion of Elizabeth and her relations with Parliament over religion, see N. L. Jones, "Religion in Parliament," in Dean and Jones, *The Parliaments of Elizabethan England*, 117–38.

5. Jones, *The Birth of the Elizabethan Age*, 26.

6. Jones, *Faith by Statute*, 130; Claire Cross, *The Royal Supremacy in the Elizabethan Church* (London: George Allen and Unwin; New York: Barnes and Noble, 1969), 19–21.

7. John Strype, *Annals of the Reformation* (Oxford: Clarendon Press, 1821), I (ii), 406–7. Heath was soon after deprived of his see and briefly committed to the Tower. Elizabeth had not forgotten, however, that Heath had proclaimed her Queen, and he was soon after set at liberty if he agreed not to publicly meddle with matters of religion, an undertaking he accepted. See *DNB*, IX, 345–6.

8. John Jewel wrote to Henry Bullinger in May 1559 that Elizabeth "seriously maintains that this honor is due to Christ alone, and cannot belong to any human being soever." Hastings Robinson, ed. and trans., *The Zurich Letters* (Cambridge: Cambridge University Press, 1846), I, 42.

9. John Guy, "Tudor Monarch and Political Culture," in Morrill, ed., *The Oxford Illustrated History of Tudor & Stuart Britain*, 22. Jones suggests that, "in terms of her prerogative, the change from headship to governorship was meaningless." Jones, *Faith by Statute*, 132. This was also recognized at the time. John Parkhurst wrote to Bullinger in May 1559: "The Queen is not willing to be called the head of the Church of England, although this title has been offered her; but she willingly accepts the title of governor, which amounts to the same thing." *Zurich Letters*, I, 38. Some Catholics also realized there was little distinction and still expressed horror over her title of Supreme Governor. Cardinal William Allen wrote in 1588, "As to her behaviour, she hath professed herself a heretic. She usurpeth, by Luciferian pride, the title of supreme ecclesiatical government, a thing in a woman unheard of, not tolerable to the masters of her own sect, and to all Catholics in the world most ridiculous, absurd, monstrous, detestable, and a very fable to the posterity." Lingard, *The History of England*, VI, 706. Of course, in calling Elizabeth "monstrous," Allen is echoing Protestant zealot Knox.

10. William P. Haugarrd, *Elizabeth and the English Reformation: The Struggle for a Stable Settlement of Religion* (Cambridge: Cambridge University Press, 1968), 129.

11. For example, over the question of the vestiarian campaign, "Parker felt that he was fighting a lone battle without support from the Privy Council or even from the Queen who had ordered him to take action . . . She also refused his request for a private royal letter to Grindal ordering him to execute the law . . . Elizabeth probably did not think it her place to order one of Parker's suffragans to obey an unequivocal command that she had already relayed to the archbishop in proper form . . . She would not subvert ecclesiastical order – even at the primate's own request . . . Parker's position was difficult. Throughout the controversy the non-conformists publicly blamed him and his bishops as if they had foisted the campaign for uniformity on the Queen." Haugaard, *Elizabeth and the English Reformation*, 219, 220. MacCaffrey argues that "at the outset of her reign [Elizabeth refused] to give her bishops of the new order the kind of royal backing they desperately needed." *Elizabeth I: War and Politics, 1588–1603*, 550.

12. Jones, *The Birth of the Elizabethan Age*, 20, 24.

13. MacCulloch, *The Later Reformation*, 28. For a discussion of Elizabeth's religious commitment, see Haugaard, *Elizabeth and the English Reformation*, viii–ix, and *passim*, Margaret Aston, *England's Iconoclasts: Volume I: Laws Against Images* (Oxford: Clarendon Press, 1988), 294–342, Scarisbrick, *The Reformation and the English People*, 110. Haigh suggests that she was not indifferent to spiritual things, and "there is some evidence of real personal commitment." *Elizabeth I*, 27.

14. Jones, *The Birth of the Elizabethan Age*, 24; Bernard, "The Church of England," 187, 188, 191.

15. Doran, *Elizabeth I and Religion*, 48. For more on Catholics in the reign of Elizabeth, see John Bossy, *The English Catholic Community, 1570–1850* (London: Darton, Longman and Todd, 1975); C. H. Aveling, *The Handle and the Axe: The Catholic Recusants in England from Reformation to Emancipation* (London: Blond and Briggs, 1976); Peter Holmes, *Resistance and Compromise: The Political Thought of the Elizabethan Catholics* (Cambridge: Cambridge University Press, 1982); Adrian Morey, *Catholic Subjects of Elizabeth I* (Totowa, NJ: Rowman and Littlefied, 1978); Patrick McGrath, *Papists and Puritans under Elizabeth I* (London: Blandford Press, 1967).

16. John Walter, "The Commons and Their Mental Worlds" in Morrill, ed., *The Oxford Illustrated History of Tudor & Stuart Britain*, 201.

17. Quoted in Doran, *Elizabeth I and Religion*, 53.

18. These events will be discussed in detail in Chapter 5 on the succession and revolts.

19. Dale Hoak, "The iconography of the crown imperial," in Hoak, ed., *Tudor Political Culture*, 91. [full essay 53–103]

20. Dudley Digges, *The Compleat Ambassador: Or Two Treaties of the intended marriage of Qu. Elizabeth of Glorious Memory: Comprised in Letters of Negotiations of Sir Francis Walsingham, Her Resident in France Together with the Answers of the Lord Burleigh, the Earl of Leicester, Sir Thos. Smith, and others Wherein, as in a clear Mirror, maybe seen the Faces of the two Courts of England and France, as they then stood: with many remarkable passages of State, not at all mentioned in any History* (London, 1655), 120, 258; *Calendar of the Letters and State Papers Relation to English Affairs Preserved in, or originally Belonging to, the Archives of Simanca*, ed. Martin Hume (London: His Majesty's Stationary Office, 1892–99), II, 410. Hereafter cited as *CSP, Spain*.

21. For more on these plots, see Chapter 5.

22. For a useful discussion of the splits within the Catholics at the end of Elizabeth's reign, see Lisa Ferraro Parmelee, *Good Newes From Fraunce: French Anti-League Propaganda in Late Elizabethan England* (Rochester, NY: University of Rochester Press, 1996), 22–5, 142–61.

23. Doran, *Elizabeth I and Religion*, 21; Regan, *Elizabeth I*, 7.

24. Haigh, *Elizabeth I*, 34.

25. J. E. Neale, *Elizabeth I and her Parliaments, 1584–1601* (New York: St. Martin's Press – now Palgrave, 1958), 74.

26. Conrad Russell, "The Reformation and the Creation of the Church of England, 1500–1640," in Morrill, ed., *The Oxford Illustrated History of Tudor & Stuart Britain*, 280, 283.

27. They were also known as "precisians," "the hotter sort of Protestants," and "the Godly."

28. Doran, *Elizabeth I and Religion*, 25.

29. Walter, "The Commons and Their Mental Worlds," 207.
30. The classic study of Puritans is Patrick Collinson, *The Elizabethan Puritan Movement* (London: Jonathan Cape, 1967). See also his *Godly People: Essays on English Protestantism and Puritanism* (London: Hambledon Press, 1983); *The Religion of Protestants: the Church in English Society, 1559–1625* (Oxford: Clarendon, 1983) and *The Birthpangs of Protestant England: Religion and Cultural Change in the Sixteenth and Seventeenth Centuries* (New York: St. Martin's Press – now Palgrave, 1988); Peter Lake, *Anglicans and Puritans?: Presbyterianism and English Conformist Thought from Whitgift to Hooker* (London: Unwin Hyman, 1988), *Protestantism and the National Church in Sixteenth-Century England* (London and New York; Croom Helm 1987), and *Moderate Puritans and the Elizabethan Church* (Cambridge and New York: Cambridge University Press, 1982).
31. Patrick Collinson, *Archbishop Grindal, 1519–1583: The Struggle for a Reformed Church* (Berkeley: University of California Press, 1979), 241; Neale, *Elizabeth and Her Parliaments, 1584–1601*, 70.
32. For more on Field, see Patrick Collinson, "John Field and Elizabethan Puritanism," in *Godly People*, 335–70.
33. Collinson, *Archbishop Grindal*, 232. Collinson's work is the classic study on Grindal.
34. Collinson, *Archbishop Grindal*, 242–5.
35. John Guy, "The establishment and the ecclesiastical polity," in Guy, ed., *The Reign of Elizabeth I*, 127–8 [entire essay 126–49].
36. Martin Marprelate was a pseudonym. The author was probably Job Throckmorton, a Puritan gentleman from Warwickshire. L. H. Carson, *Martin Marprelate, Gentleman: Master Job Throckmorton Laid Open in his Colors* (San Marino, CA: Huntington Library, 1981),
37. The Hacket case will be discussed in more detail in Chapter 5.
38. John Guy, "The 1590s? The Second Reign of Elizabeth I," in Guy, ed., *The Reign of Elizabeth I*, 11; Doran, *Elizabeth I and Religion*, 44.

3   England's Relations with Others in the First Part of the Reign

1. The major works to consult on foreign policy are those by Wernham, *The Making of Elizabethan Foreign Policy, 1558–1603*; *Before the Armada; The Growth of English Foreign Policy, 1485–1588* (London: Cape, 1966); *After the Armada: Elizabethan England and the Struggle for Western Europe, 1588–1595* (Oxford: Clarendon Press, 1984); Susan Doran, *England and Europe in the Sixteenth Century* (New York: St. Martin's Press – now Palgrave, 1999); Wallace MacCaffrey, *The Shaping of the Elizabethan Regime* (Princeton, NJ: Princeton University Press, 1968); *Queen Elizabeth and the Making of Policy, 1572–1588* (Princeton, NJ: Princeton University Press, 1981); *Elizabeth I: War and Politics, 1588–1603*.
2. Hiram Morgan, "British Policies before the British State," in Brendan Bradshaw and John Morrill, eds, *The British Problem, c.1534–1707: State Formation in the Atlantic Archipelago* (New York: St. Martin's Press – now Palgrave, 1996), 67.

3. Jane Dawson, "Anglo-Scottish protestant culture and integration in sixteenth-century Britain" in Steven G. Ellis and Sarah Barber, eds, *Conquest and Union: Fashioning a British State, 1485–1725* (London and New York: Longman, 1995), 89.

4. Wernham, *The Making of Elizabethan Foreign Policy*, 4; MacCaffrey, *The Shaping of the Elizabethan Regime*, 300.

5. D. M. Loades, *John Dudley, Duke of Northumberland, 1504–1553* (Oxford and New York: Oxford University Press, 1996), 204.

6. David Kynaston, *The Secretary of State* (Lavenham, Suffolk: Terrence Dalton, 1978), is very useful on the development of the office of the Principal Secretary.

7. Wernham, *The Making of Elizabethan Foreign Policy*, 7.

8. "Sir Thomas Smith's oration for and against the Queen's Marriage," in John Strype, *The Life of the learned Sir Thomas Smith* (Oxford, 1820), Appendix III, 186.

9. Jones, *The Birth of the Elizabethan Age*, 121.

10. Haigh, *Elizabeth I*, 11, 14; MacCaffrey, *The Shaping of the Elizabethan Regime*, 202.

11. Doran, *Monarchy & Matrimony*.

12. For a further discussion of this issue, see Levin, *The Heart and Stomach of a King*.

13. For more on the war, see C. S. L. Davies, "England and the French War, 1557–9," in *The Mid-Tudor Polity, c.1540–1560*, ed. Robert Tittler and Jennifer Loach (Totowa, NJ: Rowman and Littlefield, 1980), 159–85.

14. Morgan, "British Policies before the British State," 77.

15. When the eight years ended, however, the French simply kept Calais, though throughout the 1560s Elizabeth made sporadic efforts to get it back under English control. MacCaffrey, *Shaping*, 223.

16. D. M. Loades, *Politics and the Nation, 1450–1660: Obedience, Resistence, and Public Order* (Brighton: Harvester, 1974), 252.

17. MacCaffrey, *The Shaping of the Elizabethan Regime*, 74.

18. Dawson, "Anglo-Scottish protestant culture and integration in sixteenth-century Britain," 91.

19. Wernham, *The Making of Elizabethan Foreign Policy*, 27; MacCaffrey, *The Shaping of the Elizabethan Regime*, 90; Morgan, "British Policies before the British State," 78.

20. Wernham, *The Making of Elizabethan Foreign Policy*, 34.

21. Ferdinand died in the midst of the negotiations in 1564; they were continued by the new Emperor, Maximilian II, older brother of the Archduke Charles.

22. Palmer, *The Problem of Ireland in Tudor Foreign Policy*, 6; Morgan, "British Policy Before the British State," 80.

23. Susan Doran, "Religion and Politics at the Court of Elizabeth I: The Hapsburg Marriage Negotiations, 1559–1567," *English Historical Review*, 104 (1989), 908–26.

24. For a thorough discussion of this meeting, see Doran, *Monarchy & Matrimony*, 91–3.

25. See the discussion in Levin, *The Heart and Stomach of a King*, on Elizabeth's response to the Archduke's courtship, 53.

26. MacCaffrey, *The Making of Elizabethan Policy*, 275.

27. For the plots that involved Mary Stuart during her sojourn in England, see Chapter 5.

28. Extremely useful on the Elizabethan policy in Ireland is Nicholas P. Canny, *The Elizabethan Conquest of Ireland: A Pattern Established, 1565–76* (Sussex: Harvester, 1976; New York: Barnes and Noble, 1976); and William Palmer, *The Problem of Ireland in Tudor Foreign Policy, 1485–1603* (Rochester: The Boydell Press, 1994). See also, Colm Lennon, *Sixteenth-Century Ireland: The Incomplete Conquest* (New York: St. Martin's Press – now Palgrave, 1995); Steven G. Ellis, *Ireland in the Age of the Tudors, 1447–1603: English Expansion and the End of Gaelic Rule* (London and New York: Longman,1998). This is a revision of Ellis's earlier study, *Tudor Ireland* (1985). For a guide to the historiography of the period, see R. W. Dudley Edwards and Mary O'Dowd, *Sources for Early Modern Irish History, 1534–1641* (Cambridge: Cambridge University Press, 1985).

29. As Hiram Morgan points out, supporters of the Tudor regime would label these conflicts rebellions, but that presupposes England's legitimate control of Ireland. *Tyrone's Rebellion: The Outbreak of the Nine Years war in Tudor Ireland* (Woodbridge, Suffolk: A Royal Historical Society publication published by Boydell & Brewer, 1993), 218.

30. Palmer, *The Problem of Ireland*, 4.

31. Nicholas Harris Nicolas, *Memoirs of the Life and Times of Sir Christopher Hatton* (London: R. Bentley, 1847), 158.

32. Palmer, *The Problem of Ireland in Tudor Foreign Policy*, 90.

33. Hiram Morgan, "Hugh O'Neill and the Nine Years' War in Tudor Ireland," *Historical Journal*, 36: 1 (1993), 27–34 and *Tyrone's Rebellion*, 214–22. John Morrill cautions that there was also a crucial difference: O'Neill did not disown Tudor sovereignty; he was fighting against English domination of Irish affairs and one of his goals was the appointment of a viceroy who would sit on the English Privy Council. John Morill, "The British Problem, *c.*1534–1707," in Bradshaw and Morrill, eds, *The British Problem, c.1534–1707*, 27.

34. Palmer, *The Problem of Ireland in Tudor Foreign Policy*, 5; Morgan, "British Policies before the British State," 81.

35. Palmer, *The Problem of Ireland in Tudor Foreign Policy*, 89–90; Steven Ellis, *Tudor Ireland: Crown, Community and the Conflict of Cultures* (London, 1985), 257.

36. Digges, *The Compleat Ambassador*, 139, 164.

37. Once Henry III became king the title Anjou devolved on his younger brother, previously Alençon.

38. Wernham, *The Making of Elizabethan Foreign Policy*, 53–4. Wernham cites the Earl of Sussex: *Calendar of State Papers*, Foreign Series, XIII, 120.

39. Philip Sidney, "A discourse of Sir Philip S. to the Queenes Majesty touching hir marriage with Monsieur," in *The Complete Works of Sir Philip Sidney*, ed. Albert Feuillerat (Cambridge: Cambridge University Press,1923), III, 52.

40. MacCaffrey, *Queen Elizabeth and the Making of Policy*, 505.

41. Cited in Palmer, *The Problem of Ireland in Tudor Foreign Policy*, 99–100; and Nicholas B. Canny, *The Elizabethan Conquest of Ireland: A Pattern Established, 1565–76* (New York: Barnes and Noble Books, 1976), 121, 122.

42. Canny, *The Elizabethan Conquest of Ireland*, 122.

43. Hiram Morgan also makes the point that it is fruitful to compare "the crisis facing England in Ireland with that facing Spain in the Netherlands." Morgan, *Tyrone's Rebellion*, 15.

4   England Relations with Others in the Last Part of the Reign

1. Important work on foreign policy in the latter part of the Elizabeth's reign is MacCaffrey, *Elizabeth I: War and Politics, 1588–1603*; and Wernham, *After the Armada: Elizabethan England and the Struggle for Western Europe, 1588–1595*. Curtis Breight argues intriguingly that England meddled in the affairs of the Hapsburg Empire as a way to divert attention from problems at home and eliminate unproductive elements of society by sending them off as soldiers. *Surveillance, Militarism and Drama in the Elizabethan Era* (New York: St. Martin's Press – now Palgrave, 1996), 60. There are serious questions about Breight's argument but he raises interesting issues.
2. Kenneth R. Andrews, *Trade, Plunder and Settlement: Maritime Enterprise and the Genesis of the British Empire, 1480–1630* (Cambridge: Cambridge University Press, 1984), 11.
3. MacCaffrey, *Elizabeth I: War and Politics, 1588–1603*, 3.
4. For the assassination of William, see Motley, *Rise of the Dutch Republic*, III, 458–72; and Ridley, *Elizabeth*, 245–6.
5. For more on Ireland in this period, see Palmer, *The Problem of Ireland in Tudor Foreign Policy*; Ellis, *Ireland in the Age of the Tudors, 1447–1603*; and Colm Lennon, *Sixteenth-Century Ireland*.
6. Cited in Palmer, *The Problem of Ireland in Tudor Foreign Policy*, 113.
7. Palmer, *The Problem of Ireland in Tudor Foreign Policy*, 113–15.
8. Ellis, *Ireland in the Age of the Tudors*, 319.
9. Ridley, *Elizabeth*, 229. Ridley in addition suggests that Aubigny also became James' lover, as did Captain James Stewart, son of Lord Ochiltre.
10. Harry Kelsey, *Sir Francis Drake: The Queen's Pirate* (New Haven, CT: Yale University Press, 1998), 306.
11. For a highly readable and classic work on the Armada, see Garrrett Mattingly, *The Armada* (Boston, MA: Houghton Mifflin, 1959). An important more recent study is Colin Martin and Geoffrey Parker, *The Spanish Armada* (London: Hamilton, 1988). Another fine study is Peter Kemp, *The Campaign of the Spanish Armada* (Oxford: Phaidon, 1988). Excellent, but of more specialized interest are M. J. Rodriguez-Salgado and Simon Adams, eds, *England, Spain and the Gran Armada, 1585–1604* (Edinburgh: John Donald Publishers, 1991); and Bertrand T. Whitehead, *Brags and Boasts: Propaganda in the Year of the Armada* (Stroud, Gloucestershire; Dover, NH: Alan Sutton, 1994).
12. Kelsey, *Sir Francis Drake*, 333–4.
13. *Cabala, Mysteries of State and Government: in Letters of Illustrious Persons and Great Ministers* (London: G. Beddell and T. Collins, 1663), 373. Most historians accept that this may well have been her words, though the report of the speech is from the seventeenth century. John Neale states, "I see no serious reason for rejecting the speech," *Essays in Elizabethan History* (London: Jonathan Cape, 1958), 105. In the recent edition of Elizabeth's work, the editors accept this version of the Armada speech. *Elizabeth I: Collected Works*, ed. Marcus, Mueller, and Rose, 325. For an alternate view, see Susan Frye, "The Myth of Elizabeth at Tilbury," *Sixteenth Century Journal*, XXIII:1 (1992), 95–114.
14. Martin and Parker, *The Spanish Armada*, 14; Williams, *The Later Tudors*, 321–4.
15. Wernham, *Before the Armada*, 406.

16. Breight, *Surveillance, Militarism and Drama in the Elizabethan Era*, 114.

17. Quoted in Williams, *The Later Tudors*, 364. Williams's discussion of the issues of the French peace is valuable.

18. Very useful on this topic are Palmer, Ellis, Lennon, Morgan, and John McGurk, *The Elizabethan Conquest of Ireland: The 1590s Crisis* (Manchester: Manchester University Press 1997).

19. Ellis, *Ireland in the Age of the Tudors*, 334.

20. Morgan, *Tyrone's Rebellion*, 214.

21. Morgan, *Tyrone's Rebellion*, 214.

22. Morgan states: "This was a matter of power politics, not love. In this case Hugh O'Neill used his great personal charm to inveigle a woman half his age into his confidence and then into his bed." *Tyrone's Rebellion*, 216.

23. Ridley, *Elizabeth I*, 323.

5 Plots, Conspiracies, and the Succession

1. For discussions of the plots against Elizabeth, see Alison Plowden, *The Elizabethan Secret Service* (Hempstead: Harvester Wheatsheaf; New York: St. Martin's Press – now Palgrave, 1991); Alan Haynes, *Invisible Power: The Elizabethan Secret Services, 1570–1603* (Stroud, Gloucestershire and Wolfebore Falls, NH: Alan Sutton Publishing, 1992); and Curtis Breight, *Surveillance, Militarism and Drama in the Elizabethan Era* (New York: St Martin's Press – now Palgrave, 1996) and "'Treason doth never prosper': The Tempest and the Discourse of Treason," *Shakespeare Quarterly*, 41:1 (1990), 1–28. Much of Breight's work deals with the manufactured nature of some of the plots against Elizabeth.

2. Paul Johnson, *Elizabeth I: A Study in Power and Intellect* (London: Weidenfeld and Nocolson, 1974), 201.

3. Mortimer Levine, *The Early Elizabethan Succession Question, 1558–1603* (Stanford, CA: Stanford University Press, 1966), 7–8.

4. Levine, *The Early Elizabethan Succession Question*, 126–46.

5. Somerset, *Elizabeth I*, 105.

6. Katherine's carelessness suggests Elizabeth was correct that her cousin was not well qualified to rule, but historians generally do not doubt that the marriage had taken place. See Levine, *The Early Elizabethan Succession Question*, 21–9 for a discussion of the evidence.

7. Jones, *The Birth of the Elizabethan Age*, 106.

8. The youngest sister Mary's 1564 marriage to Thomas Keys was also treated harshly. The two were separated and Keys died in prison in 1571. Mary was then released and survived until 1578.

9. See the discussion of different historians by Jenny Wormald, *Mary Queen of Scots: A Study in Failure* (London: Collins and Brown, 1991), 15–16.

10. For more on Norfolk, see Francis Edwards, *The Marvellous Chance: Thomas Howard, Fourth Duke of Norfolk, and the Ridolphi Plot, 1570–72* (London: Hart-Davis, 1968); and Neville Williams, *Thomas Howard, Fourth Duke of Norfolk* (London: Barrie and Rockliff, 1964).

11. Christopher Haigh, *Elizabeth I*, 2nd edn (London and New York: Longman 1998), 56.

12. Wernham, *Before the Armada*, 303; MacCaffrey, *The Shaping of the Elizabethan Regime*, 320–1.

13. Plowden discusses the possibility that Ridofi was a double agent and that Burghley knew more about the plot sooner than he let on. But she does not doubt that there was a real plot. *The Elizabethan Secret Service*, 44.

14. Plowden, *The Elizabethan Secret Service*, 34.

15. For more on Morgan, see Leo Hicks, *An Elizabeth Problem: Some Aspects of the Careers of Two Exile-Adventurers* (London: Burns and Oates, 1964). Hicks makes the interesting case that Morgan was actually a double agent working secretly for Elizabeth's government, but this is not accepted by many scholars, and Hicks is unashamedly himself a supporter of Mary Stuart. See Plowden, *The Elizabethan Secret Service*, for a further discussion.

16. De Lamar Jensen, *Diplomacy and Dogmatism: Bernardino de Mendoza and the French Catholic League* (Cambridge, MA: Harvard University Press, 1964), 63.

17. Breight is highly skeptical of the Parry plot, considering it "almost undoubtedly a conspiracy manufactured by the government." *Surveillance, Militarism and Drama in the Elizabethan Era*, 255.

18. David Cressy, "Binding the Nation: the Bonds of Association, 1584 and 1696," in *Tudor Rule and Revolution: Essays for G. R. Elton from his American Friends*, ed. De Lloyd J. Guth and John W. McKenna (Cambridge: Cambridge University Press, 1982), 218.

19. See Levin, *Heart and Stomach of a King*, 111–19; and Curtis Charles Breight, "Duelling ceremonies: The strange case of William Hacket, Elizabethan messiah," *Journal of Medieval and Renaissance Studies*, 19:1 (Spring, 1989), 35–67.

20. Peter Holmes, *Resistance and Compromise: The Political Thought of the Elizabethan Catholics* (Cambridge: Cambridge University Press, 1982), 193, 209–10.

6   Culture and Difference at the End of the Reign

1. Wallace MacCaffrey, "Politics in an Age of Reformation, 1485–1585," in Morrill, ed., *The Oxford Illustrated History of Tudor and Stuart Britain*, 328.

2. Andrew Gurr, "The Theatre and Society," in Morrill, ed., *The Oxford Illustrated History of Tudor & Stuart Britain*, 156–72.

3. Leslie Fiedler, *The Stranger in Shakespeare* (New York: Stein and Day, 1965), 177.

4. Wernham, *The Making of Elizabethan Foreign Policy*, 59–60, 88–9.

5. For more on the subject, see Harold G. Fox, *Monopolies and Patents* (Toronto: University of Toronto Press, 1947); and David Harris Sacks, "The countervailing of benefits: monopoly, liberty, and benevolence in Elizabethan England," in Hoak, ed., *Tudor Political Culture*, 272–91.

6. Wernham, *The Making of Elizabethan Foreign Policy*, 88.

7. For an excellent discussion of the Parliamentary arguments, see Sacks, "The countervailing of benefits," 275–6.

8. Earlier Poor Law legislation was passed in 1536, 1552, 1563, 1572, and 1576.

9. John Guy, *Tudor England*, 326.

10. For more on the famine at this time, see Andrew B. Appleby, *Famine in Tudor and Stuart England* (Stanford, CA: Stanford University Press, 1978), 109–32.

11. Paul Slack, *The English Poor Law, 1531–1782* (Cambridge and New York: Cambridge University Press 1995), 3. See also, Paul Slack, *Poverty & Policy in Tudor & Stuart England* (London and New York: Longman, 1988).

12. Williams, *The Later Tudors*, 218; Sara Mendelson and Patricia Crawford, *Women in Early Modern England* (Oxford: Clarendon Press, 1998), 45.

13. This theory was first articulated by Keith Thomas in *Religion and the Decline of Magic* (New York: Charles Scribner, 1971).

14. *The Most strange and admirable discoverie of the three Witches of Warboys, arraigned, convicted, and executed at the last Assises at Huntington, for the bewitching of the five daughters of Robert Throckmorton, Esquire and divers others person, with sundrie Divelish and grievous torments: And also for the bewitching to death of the Lady Crumwell, the like hath not been heard of in this age* (London: Printed by the Widdowe Orwin, for Thomas Man and John Winnington, and are to be solde in Paternoster Rowe at the signe of the Talbot, 1593), no pages. All quotations are from this text. For more on the case, see Marion Gibson, *Reading Witchcraft: Stories of Early English Witches* (London and New York: Routledge, 1999), 62, 65–6, 105–7, 122–5; Barbara Rosen, *Witchcraft in England, 1558–1618* (Amherst: University of Massachusetts Press, 1991), 239–97; R. Trevor Davies, *Four Centuries of Witch-Beliefs* (London: Methuen, 1947), 32–9. Anne Barstow refers to this case as "another example of class prejudice," *Witchcraze: A New History of the European Witch Hunts* (San Francisco, CA: Pandora, 1994), 193. Catherine Belsey discusses Alice Samuel's testimony in terms of silence and language, *The Subject of Tragedy: Identity and Difference in Renaissance Drama* (London and New York: Methuen, 1985), 188–90.

15. For more on the topic, see Carole Levin, "'Murder not then the fruit within my womb': Shakespeare's Joan, Foxe's Guernsey Martyr, and Women Pleading Pregnancy in Early Modern English History and Culture," *Quidditas*, forthcoming.

16. Gibson points out that our source for this is the pamphlet, "This is a suspicious piece of noble eloquence perhaps, but it is not in the interests of the pamphleteer since it presents the witch sympathetically, and thus it may be true," *Reading Witchcraft*, 66.

17. This is the number for England suggested by Thomas, *Religion and the Decline of Magic*, 450. While the number is far smaller than on the Continent, for anyone to be executed for such a crime is a phenomenon that demands explanation.

18. See Robin Mundell, *England's Jewish Solution: Experiment and Expulsion, 1262–90* (Cambridge: Cambridge University Press, 1998).

19. Shapiro, *Shakespeare and the Jews*, 24.

20. Shapiro, *Shakespeare and the Jews*, 7.

21. C. J. Sisson, "A Colony of Jews in Shakespeare's London," *Essays and Studies*, XXIII (1937), 38. I am also deeply grateful to Charles Meyers, who shared his work on the Nuñez family, and more generally on Jews in Renaissance England, with me in manuscript.

22. Sisson, "A Colony of Jews," 40.

23. Sisson, "A Colony of Jews," 43.

24. Samuel Purchas quoted in Shapiro, *Shakespeare and the Jews*, 19.

25. William Prynne quoted in Shapiro, *Shakespeare and the Jews*, 25.

26. A point made by Robert Lacey in his discussion of Lopez and Essex, *Robert, Earl of Essex* (New York: Atheneum, 1971), 115–20.

27. David S. Katz writes extensively about Lopez and argues that Lopez was indeed guilty, *The Jews in the History of England, 1485–1850* (Oxford: Clarendon, 1994), 49–106. He also discusses the difficulties that historians have today in accepting Lopez's guilt.

28. Katz, *The Jews in the History of England*, 87, 91.

29. Katz, *The Jews in the History of England*, 100.

30. Frank Felsenstein, *Anti-semitic Stereotypes: A Paradigm of Otherness in English Popular Culture, 1660–1830* (Baltimore, MD: Johns Hopkins University Press 1995), 161.

31. For more on the sources of Titus Andronicus, see G. Harold Metz, *Shakespeare's Earliest Tragedy: Studies in Titus Andronicus* (Madison, NJ: Fairleigh Dickinson University Press, 1996), 150–3.

32. Fiedler, *The Stranger in Shakespeare*, 178.

33. For more on this issue, see also Carole Levin, "From Leo Africanus to Ignatius Sancho: Backgrounds and Echoes to *Othello*," *Lamar Journal of the Humanities*, XXII:2 (Fall 1996), 45–68.

34. James Aubrey, "Race and the Spectacle of the Monstrous in *Othello*," *Clio*, 22:3 (1993), 222.

35. William Waterman, *The Fardle of Facions conteining the auncient maners, customes and lawes of the peoples enhabiting the two parts of the earth called Affrike and Asie* (London; John Kingstone and Henry Sutton, 1555; reprinted 1888), I, 36–7, II, 10, 20–1, 21–2, 39–40.

36. Eldred Jones, *The Elizabethans and Africa* (published for the Folger Shakespeare Library by the University of Virginia, 1968), 7.

37. Richard Eden, *The First Three English books on America. [?1511]–1555 A.D. Being chiefly Translations, Compilations, etc., by Richard Eden, from the Writings, Maps, etc., of Peitro Martire, of Anghiera (1455–1526), Apostolical Protonotary, and Councillor to the Emperor Charles V; Sebastian Munster, the Cosmographer (1489–1552),Professor of Hebrew, etc., at the University of Basle; Sebastian Cabot, of Bristol (1474–1557), Grand Pilot of England: With Extracts, etc., from the Works of other Spanish, Italian, and German Writers of the Time*, Ed. Edward Arber (Birmingham, 1885), 374.

38. Eden, *The First Three English Books on America*, 376.

39. Jones, *The Elizabethan Image of Africa*, 12.

40. Morris Palmer Tilley, *A Dictionary of the Proverbs in England in the Sixteenth and Seventeenth Centuries: A Collection of the Proverbs Found in English Literature and Dictionaries of the Period* (Ann Arbor: University of Michigan Press, 1950), 473.

41. Edgar C. Knowlton, "'Indian Moors' and *Doctor Faustus*," *Cahier Elisabethains*, 23 (April 1983), 93–7.

42. As Hunter so cogently points out, *Dramatic Identities and Cultural Tradition*, 41.

43. *Oxford English Dictionary*, prepared by J. A. Simpson and E. S. C. Weiner, 2nd edn (Oxford: Clarendon Press, 1989), II, 24; 239, Hunter, *Dramatic Identities and Cultural Tradition*, 33–9; Barthelemy, *Black Face, Maligned Race*, 1–17; Winthrop Jordan, *White Over Black: American Attitudes Toward the Negro, 1550–1812* (Chapel Hill: University of North Carolina Press, 1968), 4–11.

44. F. W. Brownlow, *Shakespeare, Harsnett, and the Devils of Denham* (New York: University of Delaware Press, 1993), 341; Deborah Willis, "Shakespeare and the English Witch-Hunts," in Richard Burt and John Michael Archer, eds, *Enclosure Acts: Sexuality, Property, and Culture in Early Modern England* (Ithaca, NY, and London: Cornell University Press 1994), 112.

45. Eden, *The first Three English books on America., xix.;* Richard Hakluyt, *The Principal Navigations, Voyages, Traffiques, & Discoveries of the English Nation.* 12 vols (Glasgow: James MacLehose and Sons, 1904), VI, 137.

46. Hakluyt, *The Principal Navigations*, VI, 176.

47. Hakluyt, *The Principal Navigations*, VI, 216–19.

48. Fryer, *Staying Power*, 133.

49. In 1663 a regular slave trade began for the English with the grant of the monopoly, "The Company of Royal Adventurers of England trading with Africa," Sir Reginald Coupland, *The British Anti-Slavery Movement* (London: Frank Cass, 1933), 22.

50. W. E. Miller, "Negroes in Elizabethan London," *Notes & Queries*, n.s., VIII:4 (April 1961), 138.

51. Cited in Jones, *The Elizabethan Image of Africa*, 20–1.

52. Emeka Abanime, "Elizabeth I and Negroes," *Cahier Elisabethains*, XIX (1981), 2.

53. Heywood Townshend, diary of the Parliament, p. 263, 266, cited Sacks, "The countervailing of benefits," 284.

BIBLIOGRAPHICAL ESSAY

The number of books about Elizabeth I and her reign are legion; hundreds have been published in the last decade alone, ranging from children's books and even detective novels with Elizabeth tracking murderers at her Court to popular, lavishly illustrated texts to serious studies of specialized aspects of her reign aimed at other scholars. For students who want to pursue reading about the Queen and sixteenth-century religion, politics, and culture these are a few of the many books available, a number of which have already been listed in the notes.

The classic study of Elizabeth I is still be John Neale, *Queen Elizabeth I* (1934; rpt. Garden City and New York: Anchor Books, 1957). He is also the author of *Queen Elizabeth and Her Parliaments, 1559–1581* (London: Jonathan Cape, 1953); *Queen Elizabeth and Her Parliaments, 1584–1601* (London: Jonathan Cape, 1957). More recently, Wallace T. MacCaffrey's three books; *The Shaping of the Elizabethan Regime* (Princeton, NJ: Princeton University Press, 1968); *Queen Elizabeth and the Making of Policy, 1572–1588* (Princeton, NJ: Princeton University Press, 1981); *Elizabeth I: War and Politics, 1588–1603* (Princeton, NJ: Princeton University Press, 1992) have thoroughly explored political and diplomatic aspects of her reign. MacCaffrey crowned his achievement with his biography, *Elizabeth I* (London and New York: E. Arnold, 1993). Another scholar who has produced important work on Elizabeth is Susan Doran: *Elizabeth I and Religion, 1558–1603* (London and New York: Routledge, 1994); *Monarchy & Matrimony: The Courtships of Elizabeth I* (London and New York: Routledge, 1996); *Elizabeth I and Foreign Policy, 1558–1603* (London and New York: Routledge, 2000). For a more critical view of Elizabeth and her methods of rule, one should consult Christopher Haigh, *Elizabeth I* (London and New York: Longman, 1988). For a very different point of view, see Susan Bassnett, *Elizabeth I: A Feminist Perspective* (Oxford: Berg, 1988). Anne Somerset's biography is thorough, but accessible, and emphasizes her personal life more than her policies (New York: St. Martin's Press – now Palgrave, 1992). David Starkey's *Elizabeth: Apprenticeship* examines how Elizabeth's life prior to becoming Queen prepared her for ruling. More specialized studies of aspects of Elizabeth include Susan Frye, *Elizabeth I: The Competition for Representation* (New York: Oxford University Press, 1993); Helen Hackett, *Virgin Mother, Maiden Queen: Elizabeth I and the Cult of the Virgin Mary* (Basingstoke: Macmillan – now Palgrave, 1995), Carole Levin, *The Heart and Stomach of a King: Elizabeth I and the Politics of Sex and Power* (Philadelphia: University of Pennsylvania Press, 1994). Anyone who wants to study the Queen's own words should consult the splendid edition, *Elizabeth I: Collected Works*, ed. Leah S. Marcus, Janel Mueller, and Mary Beth Rose (Chicago, IL: the University of Chicago Press, 2000).

INDEX